GOD'S FINISHED PRODUCT

The Anointed and Chosen Women

*Explore the Hand of God As He Leads His Anointed Women
In a Peculiar Way to the Cross of Christ and Beyond*

REVEREND DR. JANET LEE SEAY-STANLEY
EPIC ANGEL ENTERPRISE BESTSELLING AUTHOR

BK Royston Publishing
Jeffersonville, IN 47131

Copyright© 2025 by Rev. Dr. Janet Lee Seay-Stanley

All Rights Reserved. No part of this book may be reproduced, stored in a retrieval system, or transmitted by any means without the written permission of the author.

Cover Design: Elite Covers

Requests for information should be addressed via email at:
Dr. Janet Seay-Stanley, janet_seay@yahoo.com

ISBN: 978-1-967282-47-0

LCCN: 2025917401

ESV – English Standard Version (ESV) - The ESV® Bible (The Holy Bible, English Standard Version®), © 2001 by Crossway, a publishing ministry of Good News Publishers. ESV Text Edition: 2025.

KJV – King James Version (KJV) - Public Domain

NIV - New International Version (NIV) - Holy Bible, New International Version®, NIV® Copyright ©1973, 1978, 1984, 2011 by Biblica, Inc.® Used by permission. All rights reserved worldwide.

NKJV - New King James Version (NKJV) - Scripture taken from the New King James Version®. Copyright © 1982 by Thomas Nelson. Used by permission. All rights reserved.

NLT - New Living Translation (NLT) - Holy Bible, New Living Translation, copyright © 1996, 2004, 2015 by Tyndale House Foundation. Used by permission of Tyndale House Publishers, Inc., Carol Stream, Illinois 60188. All rights reserved.

Printed in the United States of America

TABLE OF CONTENTS

Prologue	vii
Daddy's Girls	ix
Acknowledgements	xi
Greetings From the Author	xii
Introduction: Paradoxically Wrong. A Charismatic View	xv
PART I: GOD'S ANOINTED WOMAN!	**1**
CHAPTER 1: Distorting God's Scripture	2
History at Its Worst?	
CHAPTER 2: Women in Scripture	7
Does God Have the Right to Choose? *Unity and Harmony, Psalm 133:1* *Servant Leadership, Mark 10:45* *Effective Communication, Ephesians 4:29*	
CHAPTER 3: Anointed Women in a Toxic Environment	15
Jarena Lee, History Made by God Himself	
CHAPTER 4: He's Our Messiah, too! THE BLOODLINE	41

From the Same Cloth – Jesus' Genealogy Matthew 1:1-18
A Scholarly Article on the Inclusion of Four O.T. Women in Christ's Genealogy
With John C. Hutchinson
Survey of Explanation
An Evaluation of the Common Views/Sinners in the Messianic Line
Matthew's Intentional Inclusion of the four O.T. Women
Lies from the Early Church Fathers

CHAPTER 5: Who Says Women Can't Lead? 65

We must not hold back the righteousness that we know to tell. Romans 1:16-25
The instructions Jesus gave to "all" of us. Luke 10:1-3
Her Story

PART 2: PATTERNS OF THE FATHER 85

CHAPTER 6: *Anointed Women of God…We are God's Paradigm!* 86

With Bishop Vashti Murphy McKenzie
A "Well" Pattern of Defining Moments, John 4:3-26
A "Resurrected" Pattern of Defining Moments, Luke 24:1-11
A "Catholic Visionary" Pattern of Defining Moments
With Hildegard of Bingen

CHAPTER 7: Jesus and Women: What did Jesus Do?   117

Where Does The Church Stand in All of This?
The First Person to Whom Jesus Revealed Himself as God's Messiah was a Foreign Female. John 4:7-30
By Announcing the Resurrection Through the Testimony of Women, God Affirmed Their Role in Sharing the Good News.
Satan Attacks GOD
This is a Man's World, But It's Nothing Without a Woman or a Girl

PART 3: PROBLEM FORMATION   125

CHAPTER 8: Problem Formation   126

The Practice of Change/The Problem
A Clear Definition of the Problem in Concrete Terms
An Investigation of the Solutions Attempted So Far
Some General Research Gaps
My Research Methodology
A Clear Definition of the Concrete Change to be Achieved
The Formulation and Implementation of a Plan to Produce This Change

PART 4: BREACH OF UNITY IN CHRIST   153

CHAPTER 9: *Implementation of Our Holy Spirit*   154

Spiritual Proposal for Unified Inclusion
Signature Needed
The Public Person of the Holy Spirit
God's Calling You! The Answer, YES, to His Call!
Personal Witnesses of Their Epiphany
"Chosen to Shepherd: Discovering My True Calling"
MY CALLING BY GOD TO DELIVER HIS MESSAGE
FAITH for LIFE
CHOSEN BY GOD

Conclusion. Gamaliel Speaks. Acts 5:34-39　　183

Don't Fight Against What God has Ordained, Predestined,
Anointed, and Appointed to Help Build The Kingdom of Christ.

Bibliography (AMA style, in the order in which they appear in the text)　　187

PROLOGUE

In this phenomenal piece, the Holy Spirit points to the anointed woman, chosen by God, who has been put through the refiner's fire, brushed with the finest boar's hair, and sent to preach the unadulterated truth of Jesus Christ. This phenomenal piece of literary work is up close in 3-D. It's a tale of man's betrayal of a gift from God, a woman, a predestined helper of Christ.

Dr. Janet L. Seay-Stanley, D. Min., Christian Education Director of Jackson Street Missionary Church, a foot-soldier of God, tells a story of unsettling division and abuse by male clergy towards women in the field of righteous Christian leadership who are excluded and shunned by brothers called by God to teach love. This book is intense. It is not for the faint of heart, because God's call to men is shown in a brighter light, a light of truth.

Nevertheless, Dr. Seay-Stanley uses the Holy Spirit as her phenomenal utopia, answering the cry to bridge the gap in clergy leadership. Attached to this book is a contract, a Letter of Memorandum, to the male clergy who insist on keeping God's Word solely to themselves and keeping the truly called women silent.

DADDY'S GIRLS

I dedicate my book to my earthly father, Mr. Bobbie Lee Horton, Jr., who has four daughters in the clergy field, one way or the other, and they are:

Evangelist Terrie Nelson
(Church of God In Christ)

Reverend JoAnne Harris
(Baptist)

Exhorter Angela M. Webb
(Church of God In Christ)

Rev. Dr Janet L. Seay-Stanley
(Methodist/Baptist)

God planted His seeds, and they flourished into
God's Finished Product: The Anointed and Chosen Women
Selah

ACKNOWLEDGEMENTS

First and foremost, I thank God for sharing His knowledge with me. I am extremely thankful to all my anointed sisters in Christ, who opened up as witnesses to the verbal and mental abuse they suffered under Protestant, Jewish, or Catholic leadership from men. When I experienced and listened to your stories, they made me seek justice from a *just* God. I thank the Holy Spirit for my inspiration and for allowing me to use Him as my phenomenal utopia! We all, groups, classes, and cliques, will be unified now through the works of the Holy Spirit.

As a child, I used to say to my bullies, "I'm going to tell my daddy on you!" My earthly daddy, Bobbie Lee Horton, Jr., did not play when it came to his girls! And that's how God feels about His anointed girls/women. God does not play when it comes to His anointed female clergy! God was just waiting for me to "tell it." (LOL)

Thanks to my friend, Hazel Whitfield, my sisters, Angela M. Webb, Patricia L. Starnes, and my brother, Vincent L. Horton, for encouraging me to keep writing about things that need uncovering. Furthermore, to my ride-or-die daughters, Sharicka, LaTonya, and Yolanda, thank you for your unending support.

GREETINGS,

To the nation of called and anointed women of God who are kingdom-bound. To queens and princesses covered under God's providence, Jesus' divine resurrection and the Holy Spirit's early intervention, saved saints who are blessed to be the 'called female' from around the world, and faithful in Christ Jesus.

Attention, My Sisters in Christ:

God has acknowledged that you were 'called' according to His purpose. Called and chosen by Him into the fellowship of His Son, Jesus Christ. God called you in the 'truth.' God called you with a holy calling before time began (Romans 8:28-30; 1 Corinthians 1:4-9; 2 Thessalonians 2:14-14; 2 Timothy 1:8-9).

Beloved, remember 'whose you are,' in Christ. Some religious leaders have rejected Christ and have now turned His story around against His female messengers (Matthew 28:7-10 ESV); we are the initial mouthpiece of God in Christ Jesus.

Grace and mercy to you as you stand on the wall of faith, and peace from God our Father and the Lord Jesus Christ.

Janet L. Seay-Stanley, D. Min.—
A servant and scholar of God and the Lord Jesus Christ; an anointed and predestined woman of Jesus Christ by the will of God

INTRODUCTION

To you, anointed Israel, who are the initial love of God's heavenly plan, and the initial start of God's inspired blueprint, the Torah, God's plan of salvation, justification, deliverance, and oneness. YOU, the Jewish leaders, were the let's say, 'coup de grace' when it came to the treatment of God's women, literally. And YOU, *the Church*, born after the resurrection of our Savior, who handed you the Holy Spirit to work the works of God. Why, when you had the chance to equally lay out the sin of Adam and Eve, you distributed all the sin to Eve, and continued to mistreat and damage the reputation of females across the land and seas? From the time you were handed the mantle, you took actions and literature to end or destroy something beautiful, the anointed woman of God. Why?

Equally important, J. Lee Grady, author and ordained minister, said, we must understand that in the primitive world in which Jesus lived, women were considered little more than property. They were also viewed as evil, ignorant, and repulsively immoral. This was the view toughed by Jewish religious leaders, who did not allow women to enter parts of the temple and also segregated them from men in the synagogues. Rabbi Eliezer, who lived in Palestine in the first century, summed up Jewish rabbinical tradition when he wrote: "Rather should the words of the Torah be burned than entrusted to a woman…Whoever teaches his daughter is like one who teaches her obscenity". Another leading rabbi, Jesus' ben Sirach, summed up the Jewish position on women by saying, "He who acquires a wife gets his best possession." In other words, in Jesus' day, women were considered the source of all evil because they represented sexual temptation and the original sin of their forebear, Eve. And because they were valued only for their subservient role as wives and mothers, they were not permitted to be taught by rabbis.

As a result, after Christ's death and resurrection, the sad truth is that the church *has* lied to women about *their* worth and value in God's eyes. And I don't believe "lied" is too strong a word. Early Church fathers, and today's Church fathers, you can break with the sins of your past by admitting them. You must repent for gender prejudice. You must take responsibility for the ways you have misrepresented God and His Word to women everywhere.

PART 1: GOD'S ANOINTED WOMEN!

Chapter 1

DISTORTING THE SCRIPTURES

History is littered with examples of people who have used the Bible to justify cruelty, injustice, or bizarre behavior. Anyone can take one or two obscure verses from scripture, view them through a cultural lens, or mix them with a jaundiced personal opinion, and then build a doctrine that is totally contrary to the overall message of the Bible. Consider these examples of faulty biblical interpretation, which have caused unbelievable pain in human history.

History at Its Worst?

- The Crusaders during medieval times used biblical passages about Israel's wars with enemy nations to defend violence against Muslims. (A misreading of specific Old Testament passages can easily justify genocide.) During the crusades, Christian knights, inspired by misguided clergy, slaughtered thousands of Muslims and Jews in the name of Christ in their efforts to reclaim control of Palestine from the Turks.

- In South Africa, leaders of the Dutch Reformed Church used passages in Genesis to teach that Black people are actually animals, not humans. Then, for decades, they used sermons to support an apartheid system that denied basic human rights to Blacks in their country, sending a clear message that "the White man's God" viewed non-Whites as inferior creatures.

- In Hitler's Germany, some Christians used the Bible to defend acts of violence against Jewish people, saying that Jews deserved punishment because they were responsible for Christ's crucifixion. Today, members of the cultlike Christian Identity Movement, a racist hate group that has an estimated membership of 50,000 in the United States, use a twisted interpretation of

John 8:44-47 to suggest that Jews are products of a sexual union between Eve and Satan.

Such examples of scripture-twisting may seem extreme. But through the centuries, church leaders have distorted the Bible in similar ways to deny women the right to preach, teach, pray publicly, pursue ordination, or serve as chairpersons of mission committees. The Bible has been used to encourage women not to pursue careers other than homemaking and to teach that motherhood is a woman's only God-ordained calling in life. Ephesians 5:22 (NIV), "Wives, submit to your husbands, as to the Lord," has been used to compel Christian wives to tolerate physical or sexual abuse from their husbands to glorify God with submissive femininity.

GOD'S FINISHED PRODUCT:
The Chosen and Anointed Women…

LORD, "I want to know scripture more deeply." This is what's asked of God when you realize that you have been chosen and anointed by your *Creator,* your *Potter*, your *Defender* of life! And His answer is a given, Yes! We are God's product. Chosen women full of grace and mercy, taken through the refiner's fire, purified, polished, and full of the Holy Spirit, we are sent out to help spread the Gospel of Jesus.

As a scholar, expositor, and preacher of God's Word, I know the many trials and tribulations that men have taken anointed women of God through. And not being able to share in the spreading of the gospel or pray with our fellow Jewish/Christian brothers is questionable. However, in writing my book, inspired by the Holy Spirit, the word '*selah*' will mean stop and listen. You will see and feel the manifestation of God answering His appointed females, gifted with a Word from on high…"Let thy mercy, O Lord, be upon us, according as we hope in thee" (Psalm 33:22).

Exposit: We need thy mercy. David, an anointed man, after God's own heart, calls out "O Lord" without any partial thoughts and requests mercy "upon us." A valid request for *us,* not just the male prophets or kings or male figures, but *all* of us. David, let God know that our hope is in Him and that God is the one, the only one we have hope in, 'according to the promise which thou hast in thy word given to us'.

Application: Women of God will apply Psalm 33:22, by teaching that hope and mercy are unparalleled. They stand alone. Man will come against you, for reasons of his own, but God promised that He will go before us, and *mercy* is with Him.

Chapter 2

WOMEN IN SCRIPTURE
(No Chronological Order)

Judges 4:4-9 (ESV) "Now Deborah, a prophetess, the wife of Lappidoth, was judging Israel at that time. She used to sit under the palm of Deborah between Ramah and Bethel in the hill country of Ephraim, and the people of Israel came up to her for judgment. She sent and summoned Barak the son of Abinoam from Kadesh-Naphtali and said to Barak, "Has not the LORD, the God of Israel, commanded you, 'Go, gather your men at Mount Tabor, taking 10,000 from the people of Naphtali and the people of Zebulun. And I will draw out Sisera, the general of Jabin's army, to meet you by the river Kishon with his chariots and his troops, and I will give him into your hand'?" Barak said to Deborah, God's prophetess, "If you will go with me, I will go, but if you will not go with me, I will not go." And Deborah said, "I will surely go with you. Nevertheless, the road on which you are going will not lead to your glory, for the Lord will sell Sisera into the hand of a woman." Then Deborah arose and went with Barak to Kadesh."

Exposit: Deborah was an Old Testament prophetess; one instructed in divine knowledge by the inspiration of the Spirit of God. She judged Israel as God's mouthpiece to them; correcting abuses, and redressing grievances. By God's direction, she ordered Barack to raise an army and engage Jabin's forces. Barak insisted much upon her presence. Deborah promised to go with him. She would not send him where she would not go herself.

Application: Women of God will apply this scripture by biblically teaching the methodology of teamwork. "Therefore, encourage one another and build each other up, just as in fact you are doing" 1 Thessalonians 5:11.

Associate Pastor Witbank, of New Life Church, writes to us anointed women of God about the methodology of biblical teamwork in the workplace. We can apply ourselves with:

1. *Unity and Harmony*: Teamwork in the workplace begins with cultivating unity and harmony among team members. Psalm 133:1 says, "How good and pleasant it is when God's people live together in unity!" By embracing unity, we set aside personal agendas and work toward a common purpose, valuing the strengths and perspectives of each team member.

2. *Servant Leadership*: Jesus set the ultimate example of servant leadership, humbly teaching His disciples to serve one another. In Mark 10:45, Jesus says, "For even the Son of Man did not come to be served, but to serve, and to give His life as a ransom for many." As Christians, we should embody this servant-heartedness, seeking opportunities to support and uplift our team members.

3. *Effective Communication*: Clear and open communication is vital for effective teamwork. Ephesians 4:29 advises, "Do not let any unwholesome talk come out of your mouths, but only what helps build *others* up according to their needs, that it may benefit *those* who listen." By practicing honest and constructive communication, we foster an environment where ideas are shared, conflicts are resolved, and collaboration thrives.

Exodus 15: 19-21 "For when the horses of Pharaoh with his chariots and his horsemen went into the sea, the Lord brought back the waters of the sea upon them, but the people of Israel walked on dry ground amid the sea. Then **Miriam** the prophetess, the sister of Aaron, took a tambourine in her hand, and all the women went out after her with tambourines and dancing. And Miriam sang to them: 'Sing to the Lord, for He has triumphed gloriously; the horse and his rider he has thrown into the sea.'"

Exposit: Miriam was the first woman to be given the title of prophetess. God called on Miriam when He came down to speak with Moses and Aaron in Numbers 12:4-5. God did not exclude her to call on just the men, for He had a purpose for Miriam who aided in the deliverance of the Israelites.

Application: Women of God, apply these verses in becoming an attentive listener to God's voice that sounds like music in one's ear. The hype of this Biblical chapter is praise and dance to God's victory! The solemn singing of this song (verses 20 and 21) by Miriam or Mary (the same name) presided in an assembly of the women. They sang this song according to the softness of their sex, and the common usage of those times for expressing joy, with timbrels and dances. Moses led the psalm, and gave it out for the men, and then Miriam for the women. Famous victories were wont to be applauded by the daughters of Israel (1 Samuel 18:6, 7); so was this. When God brought Israel out of Egypt, Micah 6:4 says He sent before them Moses, Aaron, and Miriam, though we read not of anything memorable that Miriam did but this. "But those are to be reckoned great blessings to a people who assist them, and go before them, in praising God (Mt. Henry Commentary)."

2 Kings 22:8, 10, 11, 14 Verse 8, "Then Hilkiah the high priest said to Shaphan the scribe, "I have found the Book of the Law in the house of the LORD." And Hilkiah gave the book to Shaphan, and he read it. Verses 10 and 11, "Then Shaphan the scribe showed the king, saying, 'Hilkiah the priest has given me a book.' And Shaphan read it before the king. Now it happened, when the king heard the words of the Book of the Law, that he tore his clothes." Verse 14, "So Hilkiah the priest, Ahikam Achbor, Shaphan, and Asaiah went to Huldah the prophetess, the wife of Shallum the son of Tikvah, the son of Harhas, keeper of the wardrobe. And they spoke with her."

Exposit: In *A Biblical Argument for Women in Ministry and Leadership*, **Ken Schenck says,** 2 Kings 22 records a curious event in the history of Israel. The book of the law is found in the temple, probably the book of Deuteronomy. It is as if no one has been paying any attention to it for a long time (22:8,10). Josiah certainly had never read it (22:11).

Application: Here's where it gets really interesting. Neither the high priest nor the scribes around him feels qualified to seek the Lord's guidance in relation to the scriptures. Who will teach them? Who is the highest spiritual authority in the land? Is it the prophet Jeremiah or Zephaniah because they were already prophesying at this time?

No, it was a prophetess by the name of **Huldah** (2 Kings 22:14). Like Deborah, she is married, once again undermining the argument that husband headship interferes in some way with female spiritual authority. God doesn't call

Jeremiah to verify scripture. God doesn't inspire the high priest or king to speak for him. He calls a woman, the highest spiritual authority in the land. And, it doesn't matter that she is married.

Huldah is more spiritually authoritative than the high priest, and God uses her to verify scripture! God uses an inspired woman to confirm that Deuteronomy belongs in the Bible! Let that sink in.

So, when we consider Deborah and Huldah, even in the Old Testament, we find instances of women serving as the highest spiritual and political leaders of Israel. And if God did this as an exception in Old Testament times, imagine how the gates have been opened in the age of the Spirit for sons and daughters to prophesy (Acts 2:17)!

Chapter 3
ANOINTED WOMEN IN A TOXIC ENVIRONMENT

Ester 8:3-5 "Now Esther spoke again to the king, fell at his feet, and implored him with tears to counteract the evil of Haman the Agagite, and the scheme which he had devised against the Jews. And the king held out the golden scepter toward Esther. So, Esther arose and stood before the king, and said, "If it pleases the king, and if I have found favor in his sight and the thing *seems* right to the king and I am pleasing in his eyes, let it be written to revoke the letters devised by Haman, the son of Hammedatha the Agagite, which he wrote to annihilate the Jews who are in all the king's provinces."

Exposit: *Esther* was a woman who trusted God to put her in uncomfortable positions, even if that meant death. She was a fearless woman of God's plan. God anointed Esther and used her strategically to help save the Jewish people. If Esther had remained silent, out of fear or because she was told to do so, then the Jewish people might not have been delivered. Mordecai, her uncle, encouraged Esther to speak out and not be silent. There are women in the church who are afraid to speak up and be evangelists, to teach Bible studies, or use their God-given leadership skills in the church because they have been told to keep silent in these areas. The church needs more men like Mordecai to encourage women to speak truth and life to others.

Luke 1: 46-55 "And Mary said: "My soul magnifies the Lord, And my spirit has rejoiced in God my Savior. For He has regarded the lowly state of His maidservant; For behold, henceforth all generations will call me blessed. For He who is mighty has done great things for me, And holy is His name. And His mercy is on those who fear Him, from generation to generation. He has shown strength with His arm; He has scattered the proud in the imagination of their hearts. He has put down the mighty from their thrones, And exalted the lowly. He has filled the hungry with good things, And the rich He has sent away empty. He has helped His servant Israel, in remembrance of His mercy, as He spoke to our fathers, to Abraham and his seed forever."

Exposit: ***Mary,*** **the mother of Jesus**, from the New Testament, visits Elizabeth in her home in a city in Judah. While she is there, Elizabeth is pregnant with John. Mary has been chosen out of not just the women of her generation, but all of the world to bear and raise the Messiah. She found favor in God, and without hesitation or question, she had full trust in God. It is essential to remember that Mary was a very young girl and had not yet been married. Her maturity and devotion to God are incredible during this time in her life. Nijay K. Gupta said, "Though women are rarely noted as narrators, letter-authors, or speaking characters in scripture, the very fact of such a singular, pronounced, profound text like the Magnificat (Luke records) stirs the imagination to consider how she speaks eternally "the Word of God for the people of God" (Gupta 3).

Acts 18:26 "And Apollo began to speak boldly in the synagogue: whom when Aquila and Priscilla had heard, they took him unto *them*, and expounded unto him the way of God more perfectly."

Exposit: **Priscilla**, from the New Testament, was married to Aquila. Together, they were a powerful team to deliver the gospel of Jesus to others. In Acts 18:26, they are portrayed as apostles who helped a man named Apollos to be more accurate in his knowledge about Jesus. When reading in Acts, Pricilla's name is always referenced first before her husband's. Grady advises that scholars use Priscilla's name first because "Her teaching gifts were stronger and more recognized by the early church" (Grady 47). **There is no command that instructs women to have a male authority over them so that they may be permitted to disciple other people.** God often calls women into leadership roles, and if married, God does not always call the husband to do the same. **There are times that God has a greater purpose and plan for the woman. Amen.** Just like Paul, we too (anointed women) need to recognize that we are tasked with being Christ's ambassador, authorized and sent out with a divine message. We can only be effective in our mission if we are aware of our status as divine appointed witnesses.

Junia–Romans 16:7, "Greet Andronicus and *Junia*, my relatives and my fellow prisoners. They are prominent among the apostles, and they were in Christ before me." In Romans 16, Paul greets a large number of house churches. Most scholars think this chapter was greeting the churches of Rome, although some strong arguments can be made that Romans 16 was actually for the churches of Ephesus and was only grouped with Romans because he wrote both letters at the same time.

As Paul greets these churches, he mentions a husband-wife pair named Andronicus and Junia (Romans 16:7). He describes them as his "kinsmen" and "fellow prisoners." This indicates that they are Jewish believers who have been jailed for their faith. He suggests that they believed in Jesus even before he did. But the most fascinating thing he says is that they are "prominent among the apostles." To us, this is an ambiguous expression. Does he mean that they are among the apostles, or does he mean that they are well-known by the apostles? Both are possible meanings.

As a side note, the English Standard Version does not inform the reader of this choice. In keeping with its consistent bias against women in ministry, it eliminates the option in its translation. It renders the passage to say that they were "well-known to the apostles."

But this was not the understanding of the early church. Greek and Latin interpreters, such as Chrysostom, Ambrosiaster, Theodoret, and Origen, all interpreted this verse to mean that Junia was an apostle. Indeed, some copyist of the text was so uncomfortable with the implication of a female apostle that he changed the manuscript to say Junias, a male name. The Greek fathers knew Greek better than any of us in this debate, and they took Romans 16:7 to say Junia was an apostle.

The most likely reading is thus that this verse refers to a husband-wife pair as apostles. They may have been some of those apostles mentioned in 1 Corinthians 15:7– individuals to whom the risen Jesus appeared between his appearance to James and Paul. They could also have been among the 500 brothers and sisters who saw Jesus in 1 Corinthians 15:6. If Junia was an apostle, then it is "case closed" on the question of women in ministry. Apostle was the highest role in the church. If women can be apostles, then there is certainly no lesser role in which they cannot serve.

Take a moment to take that in. A married woman held the highest role in the early church – that of an apostle. If women can be apostles, then it's hard to imagine any other role that would be prohibited for them. Case closed. (Schenck, bid)

Lydia, Nympha, Junia. "From these stories, we can reconstruct a history of women working both in the church and in the marketplace for God's purposes.

Lydia and Nympha – These two women of faith opened their homes for churches to meet in. Lydia opens her home up to Paul and Silas in Acts 16:15. It is natural to assume that the church at Philippi met in her home. It is thus natural to think she was an elder in that church house. Nothing in the New Testament would prevent her – only our assumptions about what could or couldn't be.

We should note that the New Testament identifies only two people specifically as elders. 1

Peter 5:1 identifies Peter as an elder. Then the author of 2 and 3 John – traditionally identified as John – refers to himself as "the elder." It's worthwhile to take this fact into account. When someone says, "The New Testament doesn't tell us about any women being elders," it's essential to recognize that almost *no one* is explicitly identified as an elder.

We can assume that James and John were elders of the Jerusalem church (cf. Gal. 2:9). But whether you believe Mary, the mother of Jesus, or Mary Magdalene could also have been elders of the church in Jerusalem is purely a matter of your assumptions. Nothing in the New Testament would have precluded them from this role.

We can imagine the same of Nympha, who hosted a church in her home (Col. 4:15). Our assumptions make all the difference. If you assume women couldn't be elders – something the New Testament never says – you will assume Nympha was not an elder. However, suppose you observe that Paul regularly had female co-ministers and never indicated that they were only allowed to minister in certain ways. In that case, you will quite naturally conclude that Nympha was probably an overseer and an elder of the church she hosted. No mention is made of her husband. That question seemed irrelevant to the early church in terms of these roles.

Again, it is surprising that 1 Timothy 3 focuses on male elders in its instructions. The majority of elders were certainly men, but 1 Timothy also never prohibits women from being elders. That's an assumption and an argument from silence. The actual practice of the church and the theology of Pentecost suggest otherwise, especially in the earliest church when it was at its most charismatic.

Mary Magdalene – A changed servant in the Bible, forgiven by Christ. We are all the same in Christ. Mary Magdalene is often misunderstood. She was a faithful follower of Jesus. After Jesus healed her, she ventured alongside him in his ministry, meeting His needs and encouraging the disciples, eventually bearing witness to his crucifixion and burial.

Three days later, she would be the first witness to the empty tomb of Christ and one of the core critical eyewitnesses to his resurrection, which would later inspire the gospel writers to give the church historical credibility. "After the Sabbath, at dawn on the first day of the week, Mary Magdalene and the other Mary went to look at the tomb (Matthew 28:1).

Rachel waited earnestly, but patiently, to marry the love of her life: Jacob, who would later be named Israel. She was deceived by her father, Laban, and sister, Leah, who, after Jacob had worked seven years to acquire Rachel, tricked him into marrying Leah. So, Jacob worked another seven years, and Rachel waited patiently another seven years in order to marry Jacob. Although childless initially, she became the mother to Joseph, who, by God's strength, single-handedly saved all of Israel, and Benjamin, the last tribe in Israel to remain faithful to the Lord before the time of exile. Rachel's role in the history of redemption is challenging to underestimate, and she should be celebrated for her strength in the face of adversity, which is rooted in the strength of the Lord. Rachel in the Bible: "And God remembered Rachel, and God harkened to her, and opened her womb (Genesis 30:22)."

Hannah was initially childless and prayed desperately for a son. She made a promise to God that if He permitted her to bear a son, she would devote him to God. When God fulfilled this request, she faithfully kept her word. She left her son, Samuel, to be raised in the Lord's temple while continuing to provide him with guidance and mentorship along the way. Samuel, her son, would go on to rescue Israel from centuries of slavery to the Canaanites and idolatry to Baal by anointing King David. This king's heart was entirely devoted to the Lord, who also gifted God's people with most of the Psalms, which the church uses daily as a source of strength, encouragement, and worship, both through seasons of blessing and tribulation. 1 Samuel 2:10 (ESV) says, "It is not by strength that one prevails; those who oppose the Lord will be broken. The Most High will thunder from heaven; the Lord will judge the ends of the earth."

Eve is a very misunderstood character in the Bible. While she and Adam both brought sin and death into the world through partaking of the tree of the knowledge of good and evil, she is the mother of the human race. She represents God's promise to beget the one who would crush the head of the devil and redeem humanity from sin once and for all. Genesis 3:20 says, "The man called his wife's name Eve, because she was the mother of all living."

Sarah was Abraham's wife and served as an example of the fact that God always keeps His promises. When God promised Abraham he would bear a son, despite Sarah's inability to bear children,

Sarah gave birth to Isaac when she was 90 years old. Genesis 17:19 tells us, "And God said, Sarah thy wife shall bear thee a son indeed; and thou shalt call his name Isaac: and I will establish my covenant with him for an everlasting covenant, [and] with his seed after him."

Elizabeth, like Sarah, was far too old to conceive a son. However, God made it possible for her to bear a child. She would go on to conceive and give birth to John the Baptist, the last Old Testament prophet who would bear direct witness to the divinity and messianic authority of Jesus Christ. Elizabeth's faithfulness is meant to draw our minds back to Sarah and the 1,000's of years during which Israel waited for the Messiah to come. Luke 1:41 says, "And it happened, when Elizabeth heard the greeting of Mary, that the babe leaped in her womb; and Elizabeth was filled with the Holy Spirit."

Mary of Bethany was the sister of Martha and Lazarus, whom Jesus raised from the dead. She hosted Jesus in her home. While hosting Him there,

Jesus commended her for "choosing the better" by sitting at his feet instead of being distracted by housework and the duties of entertaining. Mary of Bethany represents Jesus' clear message that He cuts through cultural expectations and desires to extend fellowship to all human beings, despite the hierarchy humans are often tempted to establish, which marginalizes and suppresses others. In John 12:1-8, we read this account. "Then, six days before the Passover, Jesus came to Bethany, where Lazarus was who had been dead, whom He had raised from the dead. There they made Him a supper; and Martha served, but Lazarus was one of those who sat at the table with Him. Then Mary took a pound of very costly oil of spikenard, anointed Jesus' feet, and wiped them with her hair. And the house was filled with the fragrance of the oil. But one of His disciples, Judas Iscariot, Simon's son, who would betray Him, said, "Why was this fragrant oil not sold for three hundred denarii* and given to the poor?" This He said, not that He cared for the poor, but because he was a thief, and had the money box; and he used to take what was put in it. But Jesus said, "Let her alone; she has kept this for the day of My burial. "For the poor you have with you always, but Me you do not have always."

Martha, the sister of Mary, was rebuked by Jesus for putting her entertainment obligations above learning the words of Jesus. However, she was still a devoted disciple of Christ and deeply desired to know and love Jesus, doing everything in her power to dignify Him as the unknown King. Here's the biblical account: "Now it happened as they went that He entered a certain village; and a certain woman named Martha welcomed Him into her house. And she had a sister called Mary, who also sat at Jesus' feet and heard His word. But Martha was distracted with much serving, and she approached Him and said, 'Lord, do You not care that my sister has left me to serve alone? Therefore, tell her to help me.' And Jesus answered and said to her, 'Martha, Martha, you are worried and troubled about many things. But one thing is needed, and Mary has chosen that good part, which will not be taken away from her' (Luke 10:38-42)."

Jehosheba was the daughter of King Joram. She is known for saving her nephew while he was an infant. Her nephew was the Prince Joash, who was to be massacred by the Queen Mother. Joash's survival enabled the line of David, and consequently the line of the Messiah, to endure. Jehosheba's bravery played a critical role in the possibility of the coming of Christ, and God's working through her faithful devotion to his purposes is difficult to underestimate. We read her story in 2 Kings 11:2, "But Jehosheba, the daughter of King Joram, sister of Ahaziah, took Joash the son of Ahaziah, and stole him away from among the king's sons who were being murdered; and they hid him and his nurse in the bedroom, from Athaliah, so that he was not killed."

Rebekah was the wife of Isaac and the mother of twin sons, Esau and Jacob. Rebekah's story is intricately linked with God's divine plan for the lineage of Abraham. Notably, she was chosen as Isaac's wife after a servant of Abraham prayed for guidance, and she showed kindness by offering water to him and his camels. Later in life, Rebekah played a pivotal role in ensuring that Jacob, the younger son, received Isaac's blessing, which had significant implications for the future of the Israelite nation. Genesis 24:15 tells us, "And it happened, before he had finished speaking, that behold, Rebekah, who was born to Bethuel, son of Milcah, the wife of Nahor, Abraham's brother, came out with her pitcher on her shoulder."

Leah was the elder daughter of Laban and the first wife of Jacob. Though Jacob's heart was set on marrying Rachel, Leah's younger sister, Laban deceived him into marrying Leah first. Despite being less favored than Rachel, Leah became the Mother of six of Jacob's sons, including brothers Levi and Judah, from whom the priestly and royal lines of Israel would descend, respectively.

Throughout her life, Leah sought love and validation, and her story is one of resilience and God's favor in unexpected places. Genesis 29:31 says this about Leah, "When the LORD saw that Leah was unloved, He opened her womb; but Rachel was barren."

There are times that God has a greater purpose and plan for the woman; amen. Just like Paul, we need to recognize that we are tasked with being Christ's ambassadors, authorized and sent out with a divine message. We can only be effective in our mission if we are aware of our status as divinely anointed and appointed witnesses of Christ.

Romans 16: 1-2 "I commend unto you *Phebe* our sister, who is a servant of the church which is at Cenchree: That ye receive her in the Lord, as becometh saints, and that ye assist her in whatsoever business she hath need of you: for she hath been a succorer of many, and of myself also (KJV)."

Exposit: Phoebe from the New Testament was a deacon and minister of her time, instructed by Paul to go to Rome and be an evangelist and help in rooting new churches. In Romans 16:1, Phoebe is referred to as a servant. When examining Paul's Greek dialect, he uses the word diakonon, which is the Greek word for "deacon." Diakonon is also the same word to describe other deacons of the Bible who were men like Stephen and Philip (Grady 46)… It is safe to say that Phoebe also belonged in the same category as these men. Grady said, "Deacons in the New Testament were often powerful ministers who worked miracles when they preached" (Grady 47). Considering that Phoebe held such a powerful role as a deacon anointed by God, there is no sense as to why that role was acceptable then but not in today's generation of women. "I suspect that some men were jealous of women's God-filled-power."

In his book *"Christ-Centered Exposition,"* Tony Merida states that Phoebe heads the list.

Phoebe is the first woman mentioned. She probably carried the letter to Rome. Paul calls her a "benefactor" (v. 2). This means she was a person of means and maturity. It seems she had the necessary resources to travel to Rome. Phoebe is, then, a great example of how wealthy Christians should use their resources: for the good of the church and the expansion of the gospel.

There is considerable debate about whether Phoebe was a deacon in Cenchreae (the port of Corinth), but I am not going to dive into that discussion, as it has many layers to it. So, it is impossible to know for sure. But the addition of "of the church in Cenchreae" probably indicates some kind of position in the church, and it at least highlights the fact that *she is well known for her service in the church.* She is an exemplary saint, and Paul wants the church to receive her warmly.

NOTE: Into the nineteenth century, God continued to anoint women and have a great purpose for them. Two women, Catherine Booth and Jarena Lee, have been recorded in history as co-founders of the Salvation Army. Doriani said, "In Booth's view, when Deborah, Huldah, Miriam, and Anna ministered beside men, they also preached" (Doriani, 164). She had a strong belief that women were allowed to prophesy and preach. She believed that a woman's place was not solely in the home, but also out preaching God's word to everyone.

Jarena Lee, History Made by God Himself

Jarena Lee was an African American woman who began as an exhorter and later started preaching in 1819 to racially mixed congregations. Lee explains in her personal journal that she heard a voice tell her to "Go preach the gospel." She thought that people would not believe her if she followed this instruction. She even thought that what she heard may have been Satan's deceiving words being spoken to her. She prayed to God for clarity and found a Bible lying on a pulpit. Lee found her clarity, and from that day on, she was obedient in the Lord (*Religious Experience and Journal of Mrs. Jarena Lee*). Lee believed that women had the same right to preach as men. She replied with a powerful statement to the idea of women preaching being an improper act. She had believed that they had every right to preach. Lee stated, "The Savior died for the woman as well as the man. If a man may preach because the Savior died for him, why not the woman, seeing that he died for her, also? Is He not a whole Savior instead of a half one?" (Wigger 153)? Lee is making it clear that she believes Jesus did not hold one gender higher than the other, but rather gave men the authority to go out and preach His gospel. Lee devoted her life to preaching and traveling America to deliver the message. In 1835, she devoted herself to traveling over 700 miles, spreading the gospel (Wigger 153).

Moreover, I am in agreement with Cindy Sears, *Anointed Women and Their Role in Ministry,* October 18, 2015, when she continues to voice powerful views that, "The ideology that it is only acceptable for men to hold leadership positions and be the head of the church is incorrect. Churches have taken Paul's letters and picked certain sections of his words, and have read them at face value. There are times when taking his words at face value will twist what Paul wanted to convey. There were times when Paul targeted specific issues in the church that needed correction. There are other factors that are to be taken into consideration when reading Paul's letters to rule out contradiction. Three of these factors are the original written dialect, culture, and reading the full context.

The Apostle Paul wrote a letter to both women and men in the church, providing them with guidance on their behavior. Paul said, "A woman must quietly receive instruction with entire submissiveness. But I do not allow a woman to teach or exercise authority over a man, but to remain quiet (1 Timothy 2:11-12 NIV)." In this context, obvious instructions appear to be black and white. However, this scripture in the book of Timothy has been misused for its face value to silence women. Paul cannot be making a broad statement in meaning that all women cannot teach over a man. In Acts, Paul speaks about Priscilla and Aquila. Priscilla aided in correcting Apollos' biblical teachings. In 2 Timothy 1:9, Paul praises Lois and Eunice for the instruction they gave to Timothy. By Paul giving high praise to these women, Paul clearly did not mean that teaching is not allowed to all women. To believe that Paul meant all women should remain quiet does not make sense. Joel said, "Then, after doing all those things, I will pour out my Spirit upon all people (Joel 2:28 NIV)."

Chapter 4

HE'S OUR MESSIAH TOO! THE BLOODLINE

From the Same Cloth—Jesus' Genealogy

Jesus' genealogy, in Matthew 1:1-18 (NLT), gives women the ultimate inclusivity of God's comprehensive plan.

"The book of the genealogy of Jesus Christ, the son of David, the Son of Abraham: Abraham begot Isaac, Isaac begot Jacob, and Jacob begot Judah and his brothers. Judah begot Perez and Zerah by Tamar, Perez begot Hezron, and Hezron begot Ram. Ram begot Amminadab, Amminadab begot Nahshon, and Nahshon begot Salmon. Salmon begot Boaz by Rahab, Boaz begot Obed by Ruth, Obed begot Jesse. Jesse was the father of King David. David was the father of Solomon (whose mother was Bathsheba, the widow of Uriah). Solomon was the father of Rehoboam. Rehoboam was the father of Abijah. Abijah was the father of Asa. Asa was the father of Jehoshaphat. Jehoshaphat was the father of Jehoram. Jehoram was the father of Uzziah. Uzziah was the father of Jotham. Jotham was the father of Ahaz. Ahaz was the father of Hezekiah. Hezekiah was the father of Manasseh. Manasseh was the father of Amon. Amon was the father of Josiah. Josiah was the father of Jehoiachin and his brothers (born at the time of the exile to Babylon). After the Babylonian exile, Jehoiachin was the father of Shealtiel. Shealtiel was the father of Zerubbabel. Zerubbabel was the father of Abiud. Abiud was the father of Eliakim. Eliakim was the father of Azor. Azor was the father of Zadok. Zadok was the father of Akim. Aakim was the father of Eliud. Eliud was the father of Eleazar. Eleazar was the father of Matthan. Matthan was the father of Jacob. Jacob was the father of Joseph, the husband of Mary. Mary gave birth to Jesus, who is called the Messiah. All those listed above include fourteen generations from Abraham to David, fourteen generations from David to the Babylonian exile, and fourteen from the Babylonian exile to the Messiah. This is how Jesus the Messiah was born. His mother, Mary, was engaged to be married to Joseph. But before the marriage took place, while she was still a virgin, she became pregnant through the power of the Holy Spirit."

A Scholarly Article of the Inclusion of Four Old Testament Women in Christ's Genealogy

John C. Hutchison, Associate Professor of Bible Exposition, sheds much-needed light on the topic of women's marginalization. The surprising inclusion of the names of four Old Testament women in Christ's genealogy has generated much discussion by those who recognize the typical genealogical form used in Matthew 1:1-18.

Though the reference to Tamar, Rahab, Ruth, and "the wife of Uriah" provides historical information that is not part of the genealogy proper, the mention of these particular matriarchs and not others seem to be an intentional and significant feature of Matthew's portrayal of the Messiah. Why did Matthew include the names of four women in a patriarchal genealogy of the Messiah? And why did he choose these women and no other more prominent matriarchs?

Most biblical expositors have approached these questions with the assumption that Matthew cited these names because they share something in common about the messianic mission. Some emphasize that their Gentile ancestry foreshadows Jesus' concern for Gentiles in the church. Others say that the immorality in each of the women's lives foreshadows God's forgiving grace or was cited to soften the scandal that arose over Mary's unwed pregnancy. Most of the explanations that seek to establish a common thread between the women, however, seem to force the issue.

Explanations sometimes ignore the biblical theology of the book and fail to relate the use of these names to Matthew's purpose as a Gospel writer.

This thesis, presented in this article, is that Matthew intentionally cited four Old Testament women in his genealogy to bring attention not to four persons, but to four familiar Old Testament stories that illustrate a common point. The allusions span the Old Testament periods of the patriarchs, the conquest, the judges, and David's kingdom, and in each case, a Gentile shows extraordinary faith in contrast to the Jews, who were greatly lacking in their faith. The faith of Tamar versus that of Judah, of Rahab versus that of the Israelites in the wilderness, and of Ruth versus that of the Judges generation illustrates that at crucial times in Israel's history, Gentiles demonstrated more faith than Jews in response to God. Bathsheba is probably cited by Matthew as "the wife of Uriah" in order to focus attention on Uriah's faith in contrast to that of David.

Through all of this, God remained faithful in preserving the messianic line, and in some cases, He did it through godly Gentiles. These contrasts are consistent with Matthew's purpose to remind Jews of God's faithfulness to His Abrahamic and Davidic kingdom, and to exhort them to forsake the self-righteous attitude of many Jews toward Gentiles who were now joining them in the church. Matthew accomplished this by reminding them of the crucial role Gentiles played in the messianic story.

Survey of Explanations

Several scholars have looked for a common thread in the lives of the four Old Testament women. As Weren writes, "The gospel according to Matthew begins with a list of Jesus' ancestors in which the names of five women occur among those of forty-two men. Mention of Mary is not surprising, because she is Jesus' mother, but why does the author include four other women: Tamar, Rahab, Ruth, and the wife of Uriah (Bathsheba)? There are various answers to this question. Usually, the exegetes look for something which the four Old Testament women have in common, while Mary is not taken into consideration."

Others have proposed a common thread that might also explain the mention of Mary in verse 16. As Nolland observes, "The place of the four women (five counting Mary) in the Matthean genealogy has been much explored. The central drive of most of the investigation has been to find a common denominator among the four women, and if possible, one that can also encompass Mary. Occasionally, one notes a disgruntled expression of disbelief in any significant commonality, but this has not dimmed the enthusiasm of those who seek to demonstrate one kind of commonality or another.

The four most common views are as follows. First, the *inclusion* of the four Old Testament women highlights their background as sinners and God's grace in accepting them. This view, probably first espoused by Jerome, focuses on the sinful background of the women in order to foreshadow the Messiah's role in saving His people from their sins and to demonstrate God's grace and sovereignty in fulfilling the Davidic promise despite human failure. "The God about whom Jesus taught had shown Himself ready, in the history of the royal family, to accept strangers and sinners."

Second, the *inclusion* of the women celebrates the *inclusion* of Gentiles in Messiah's genealogy and mission. This view, popularized by Martin Luther, focuses on women as Gentiles in anticipation of *the Great Commission*, in which Jesus is seen as more than just a Jewish Messiah. This viewpoint contends that since Matthew's Gospel cites Gentile blood in the Messiah's line, it would have had appeal to them. In addition, Christ's message would have reminded Jews of the universal messianic message. In Matthew 28, the resurrected Christ declares, "All authority in heaven and on earth has been given to me." Thus speaks the son of David, in whom the covenant with David is fulfilled. In the following verses, he commands,

"Go therefore and make disciples of all nations, baptizing …teaching them to observe all that I have commanded you." A scriptural basis is thus indicated for the missionary outreach of the church, which is commanded to become involved in fulfilling that which has been God's purpose since the call of Abraham. That such an allusion is intended is indicated by the *inclusion* of the foreign women, Tamar, etc., in the genealogy.

Third, the Old Testament women, like Mary, all had unusual marital situations and even sexual scandals in their past. Each woman either took action or was divinely used to further God's providential plan for His people. This variation of the first view focuses not so much on the women's sinful background as on the scandalous circumstances of each woman, who showed initiative or played an important role in God's plan. In this view, the women are mentioned as a response to the public scandal about Mary's supposedly illegitimate child, whose story appears immediately after the genealogy in Mathew's account. The mention of the women would have been an encouragement to early Jewish Christians, who were faced with the argument by unbelievers that the Messiah's birth was scandalous. This view is held by Raymond Brown and Edwin Freed. Brown, who presents one of the best formulated statements of this view, explains, "It is the combination of the scandalous or irregular union and of divine intervention through the woman that explains best Matthew's choice in the genealogy." He then observes that in later Judaism, the behavior of these women was actually thought to have been guided by the Holy Spirit. Weren also relates the four Old Testament women *to Mary as significant instruments of God at crucial points in Israel's history.*

My theory is that Mary continues in a role that Tamar, Rahab, Ruth, and Bathsheba already played in the stories from the Hebrew Bible. What is said here about Mary is also important in addressing the question of why Matthew includes four more women in his list of Jesus' ancestors. The way in which the four women figure there sheds in turn some more light on Mary's position. I will argue that those stories reveal how Israel's history would have been cut short prematurely had these women not seen it as their task to map out alternative pathways to the future. The first chapter of Mathew tallies with this idea. He sees Jesus as the purpose of Israel's history. Still, this history has achieved its aim not through the efforts of men, but through the extraordinary, concerted action of *female forces*.

Chazal projects a contemporary theme of the powerlessness of women back into these stories. "These women, Tamar, Rahab, Ruth, and Bathsheba, all without power as women, acted quite out of keeping with the ideas of their day as to the position of women. They acted to *fulfill God's will*."

Fourth, the inclusion of the women reveals Matthew's defense of the Davidic messianic viewpoint in contrast to those who supported a priestly line. This view, advanced by Johnson, is not widely held, but it does introduce the element of an intra-Jewish debate over the ancestry of the Messiah. In this view, Matthew shared the viewpoint of the Pharisees of his time that the Messiah had come from Davidic roots, which included scandal and Gentile blood. This would indicate that Matthew believed that Jesus fulfilled Pharisaic messianic expectations and that Matthew disagreed with those who believed in a priestly messianic line.

An Evaluation of the Common Views/Sinners in the Messianic Line

The explanation that women were sinners in Christ's genealogy does not accurately represent the biblical presentation and emphasis in the stories of the four Old Testament women. Nor does it take into consideration the Jewish perception of these matriarchs at the time Matthew wrote his Gospel.

Every person in Christ's genealogy was a sinner, and others, such as Ahaz (Matthew 1:9, Manasseh (verse 10), and even Judah verse 3), engaged in more scandalous sins in Israel than any of the *women*. Also, not all of the four women could be considered scandalously sinful. Certainly, Tamar and Bathsheba were guilty of sexual sins, but neither of them is depicted as bearing the most incredible guilt. Judah's admission of guilt–"She is more righteous than I" (Genesis 38:26)–indicates that he recognized her motives as purer than his own. Though she resorted to an act of sexual immorality, Tamar's motives were focused on the continuation of Judah's family line. The central problem was Judah's wicked and disobedient sons, Er and Onan (verses 6-14), and Judah's refusal to offer his third son, Shelah (verse 14), which might have prevented the continuation of the messianic line of Judah. *Tamar* devised a plan to rectify the problem. In addition to the Judah-Tamar contrast, Genesis 38-39 seems to contrast the immoral and self-righteous actions of Judah with the impeccable character of Joseph. Thus, the Genesis narrative highlights the sins of Judah and his family, not those of *Tamar*.

In a similar fashion, the David-Bathsheba story focuses on David's sin, not on the guilt of Bathsheba. When David decided to pursue her, he was the one who was where he should not have been (2 Samuel 11:1), and she presumably had no sinful intentions. David pursued her with the absolute power of an oriental king, who could expand his harem at will. The intended contrast in the narrative is between David's sins of adultery, deceit, and murder, and Uriah's integrity, with essentially no emphasis on Bathsheba's sin. This may be the reason Matthew referred to her as "the wife of Uriah."

One can be even more dogmatic about the absence of sexual sins in the Old Testament accounts of Rahab and Ruth. While Rahab's past as a prostitute is mentioned, there is no hint of further immoral behavior after her profession of faith in the Lord (Joshua 2:8-21). The label "prostitute," identifying her immoral past, was intended to provide a contrast in the story to her amazing conversion. She is also cited in Hebrews 11 and James 2 as an example of a believer who took action in response to faith. Although some have accused Ruth of immoral behavior with Boaz, there is no evidence of this in the Old Testament narrative account.

The quest to find a common denominator in these four stories has sometimes led biblical expositors to make overly generalized evaluations of the four women. The women were not shining lights of moral integrity. Tamar (Genesis 38), Canaanite wife of Er, son of Judah, disguised herself as a prostitute in order to seduce her father-in-law, Judah, so that she could have children. Rahab was a professional prostitute in ancient Jericho and sheltered the spies sent there by Joshua (Joshua 2:2-21). In return, the Israelites saved her life when they captured the city (Joshua 6:22-25). Ruth, a Moabite girl, showed virtuous conduct in that she loved and remained loyal to her mother-in-law, a Hebrew woman. But Ruth probably lost her virtue one night at a party during the grain festival when she crawled under the covers with Boaz, who later became her husband (Ruth 3). The fourth woman, the wife of Uriah the Hittite (Bathsheba), took a bath at just the right time, "spring of the year," and in the right place to be seen by David as he strolled on the roof of the palace. She later became pregnant by David, who then had her husband killed in battle to make his marriage to her easier (2 Samuel 11-12).

After this sordid (and in my estimation inaccurate) characterization, Freed makes an important observation. "However, the Jewish Christians to whom Matthew was writing no longer thought of those women as sinners but as heroines. There is evidence that in Judaism, they had come to be regarded as distinguished women because each had done something beneficial to the Jewish people." Freed then traces the reputation of these women in post-New Testament Jewish literature, citing numerous examples from the Talmud and Midrash, as well as Philo and Josephus, which share the same views on their honored status. Davies agrees with this favorable assessment, as does Brown.

In weighing this understanding of the women, we should note, however, that the Bible does not make all these Old Testament women sinners. It is not clear, for instance, that Ruth sinned with Boaz. Moreover, while in the Old Testament the other women were guilty of unchastity in varying degrees, in the Jewish piety of Jesus' time, these women came off quite well. Tamar was esteemed as a saintly Jewish proselyte; for by her initiative, she had perpetuated the family line of Judah's son. She is said to have done this because she had faith in the messianic promise concerning Judah's lineage, and she wanted to share in its blessing. Rahab, also classified as a proselyte, was looked on as [a] heroine for having helped in Israel's victory at Jericho; and in early Christian writing she was hailed as a model of faith (Hebrews 11:31); 1 Clement 12:1). Even Bathsheba's adultery was not always condemned in rabbinic literature because she ultimately gave birth to Solomon. Thus, there is little likelihood that Matthew's readers would have understood the women as sinners. Some who agree that Ruth is not pictured as immoral in the Book of Ruth point instead to the fact that she was a Moabite and thus a descendant of Lot from his sin of incest with his daughters (Genesis 19:30-37). This would seem, however, to be grasping for a common denominator where one does not exist.

One must seriously doubt that these women were viewed with disdain in the New Testament period and beyond. This fact is essential, for the meaning attached to Matthew's choice of matriarchs would certainly have been consistent with the common perception of these women in his day. *Selah*

Based, therefore, on the information in all four Old Testament accounts and the probable perception of the four women in Matthew's day, the viewpoint that emphasizes their sinful character or behavior is simply not adequate.

Matthew's Intentional Inclusion of the Four Old Testament Women

Women were not usually included in Jewish genealogies. In addition, Matthew's departure in chapter 1 verses 3, 5, and 6 from the consistent "A was the father of B" formula implies that the matriarchal information is intentional and purposeful. After all, the genealogical statements would have been complete without these parenthetical comments. Perhaps Matthew received his inspiration from the inclusion of Tamar's name in 1 Chronicles 2:4. Still, his choice to include not one, but four similar citations would seem to indicate a greater purpose. The organization of his genealogy in a three-by-fourteen arrangement, which omits many generations, suggests that he was committed to a concise and organized approach; additionally, including the names of mothers in Jewish genealogies is quite rare. While Matthew 1:1-18 includes four other aberrations from the genealogical formula, each of the others can be explained more easily.

In addition, Grady asked the question, "Are Women Second Class?" Male pastors, Priests (Jesus was the last Priest, like Melchizedek), Monarchs, Popes, and Archbishops have stagnated females from preaching the Gospel of Jesus Christ since the Early Church started! We refuse to stop preaching the death, burial, and resurrection of Jesus Christ! Relatively speaking, Grady continues to say, "Mission agencies in England told Gladys Aylward that she would never be an effective minister in China. In the 1930s, British women were rarely sent to the foreign field to preach; females could go as missionaries only if they were school teachers or nurses." Men should not continue to hinder women from preaching the Gospel of Christ! We all fall under the 'Blood of Christ,' not just menfolk.

The "Church of Christ" must move in a forward manner, not stagnate by some jealous and envious religious men. You see, Gladys wasn't a teacher or a nurse, but she couldn't resist the call of God. Women who speak or preach the gospel were pre-destined by God, as well as men. Nothing in this world goes on without God's knowledge. And if those male figures knew God and His Word, they would not hinder women from spreading the Gospel of Christ. Just listen to some negative and outright lies from the early church fathers to today's pastors: ***God maintained the order of each sex by dividing the business of life into two parts, assigning the more necessary and beneficial aspects to men and the less important, inferior matters to women.***
<u>EARLY CHURCH FATHER</u> John Chrysostom <u>(A.D. 347-407)</u> - *A woman's intellect usually is feebler, and her curiosity greater than that of a man.*

Women should not govern the state or make war or enter the sacred ministry. Thus, they can dispense with some of the more difficult branches of knowledge which deal with politics, the military arts, jurisprudence, philosophy, and theology. Their bodies as well as their minds are less strong and robust than those of men.

<u>FRANCOIS DE SALIGNAC DE LA MOTHE-FENELON IN THE EDUCATION OF FEMALES PUBLISHED IN THE LATE SEVENTEENTH CENTURY -</u> *Women have no call to the ballot-box. Still, she has a sphere of her own, of amazing responsibility and importance. She is the divinely appointed guardian of the home. She should therefore fully realize her position is the holiest, most responsible, and queenlike assigned to mortals; and dismiss all ambition for anything higher, as there is nothing else here so high for mortals.*

FUNDAMENTALIST LEADER JOHN MILTON WILLIAMS IN WOMEN'S SUFFRAGE (1893), WHICH USED THE BIBLE TO OPPOSE THE MOVEMENT TO GIVE WOMEN THE RIGHT TO VOTE - *We don't believe there's a place for women elders in the church.* **When the apostle Paul said that a woman should not "teach or exercise authority over a man" (1 Timothy 2:12), he did not follow that statement with a cultural argument. Instead, he went all the way back to creation to show that women weren't intended to dominate men. The reasons he gave are that the woman was created after the man and that she was deceived when acting independently of his leadership.** CALIFORNIA PASTOR AND AUTHOR JOHN MACARTHUR, IN A STATEMENT ON WOMEN POSTED ON HIS *GRACE TO YOU* WEBSITE - Again, "It is also essential for us to recognize that even though Jesus selected twelve Jewish males to lead the early church, He was in no way signaling that future leaders of the church must be Jewish. To the contrary, the Holy Spirit showed the early disciples that the gospel was also sent to the Gentiles, and within a few years, Gentile apostles emerged. Thus, we must see that just because the first apostles were male, this does not set a precedent for all time. Women, including Priscilla and Junia, were already functioning in fivefold ministry roles by the time the early church began penetrating Europe and Asia Minor.

Chapter 5

WHO SAID WOMEN CAN'T LEAD?

Jackie Rodriguez, a Florida housewife and mother of one small child, began accepting invitations to preach in churches in her city. Her husband, Nuno, a pastor in Orlando, was baffled by his wife's decision to step out and assume such a high-profile role. But Jackie never once asked for a speaking engagement. Churches called her and begged her to minister. "I didn't ask to do this," she told Nuno once when he questioned her motives. "I have not once picked up the telephone and called anyone to ask them to schedule me. God is opening these doors."

It was not an easy road for Jackie. In Hispanic culture, where *machismo* is a dominant force, women are expected to function in a purely domestic role. And Jackie soon found that machismo is also a powerful influence in Hispanic churches. When pastors heard her speak, they were shocked. She spoke with authority, but they could not reconcile her obvious anointing with the cultural traditions that held a vice-grip on their minds. To them, Jackie was violating an unwritten law of Spanish culture. "Who do you think you are?" pastors would ask her. "You are coming across too strong. You are a woman!" they would scream. Some of the Hispanic women also opposed her, but Jackie pressed through the resistance and ultimately gained respect. Looking back on her earliest years in ministry, Jackie realizes that she had to oppose a stronghold of prejudice. "We Hispanic women have been under slavery," she says now. "The Hispanic pastors told women that they should be quiet. They told them to show up at church and then to shut up!"

Jackie no longer fights this battle every day. In 1999, she and her husband became associate pastors at The Church of the People, a twelve-hundred-member Hispanic Charismatic congregation in Mission, Texas, on the far eastern border of Mexico. Jackie began preaching sermons and airing a Spanish-language broadcast, *Waves of Revival*, that reaches thousands in the Mexican cities of Reynosa and Matamoros. She also began broadcasting to the entire region a television program featuring her relevant preaching. And people started responding to her message.

There are some leaders in the church today who would say that Jackie Rodriguez's ministry is illegitimate. If they could, they would yank her off the podiums and platforms where she stands and pulled her TV and radio programs off the airwaves because they believe her gender disqualifies her from carrying the message of the gospel (Grady 51). How did they arrive at such a warped conclusion?

As much as men want to believe, there is no biblical basis for the idea that women cannot raise their voices against injustice, challenge sin in the church, or call sinners to repentance. There is no scriptural requirement that when women pray, prophesy, lead worship, teach seminars, establish new churches, start drug rehabilitation centers, minister in prisons, or preach sermons, they must do it less passionately than men. Why then do so many Christians, even in the twenty-first century, still believe that women who proclaim God's Word boldly are either "masculine" or "out of order." On more than one occasion, Grady said that he even heard that ministers snidely suggest that women who preach in an authoritative style must be lesbians–because, they say, they "want to do a man's work."

We need to understand that the Bible does not lock women into the stereotypical mold of silent wimps. God does not set limits on the volume level of a woman's voice. In Proverbs, godly wisdom is portrayed as a fearless woman who stands in the middle of the city and "cries out" with a loud voice. (See Proverbs 8:1-11). She declares, "To you, O men, I call, and my voice is to the sons of men" (verse 4). Not only does she preach authoritatively, but she also preaches to men. This allegorical woman is not leading a women's Bible study in her home. She is evangelizing men in the central square of a major city. Yet how many leaders of major denominations in the United States would tell this woman preacher to sit down and shut up?

As previously stated, Catherine Booth, co-founder of The Salvation Army, was often criticized by the male clergy of her day because she conducted a public ministry and provided strong leadership to her evangelistic organization. Her detractors often used the argument that it was "against nature" for a woman to preach because God created females to be weak, gentle, and subservient. Mrs. Booth pointed out in her most famous 1859 treatise, *Female Ministry: Woman's Right to Preach the Gospel,* that objections to women in the pulpit were purely because of cultural biases and traditions.

In the rigid Victorian culture that Mrs. Booth challenged, women were viewed as delicate, decorative ornaments. They were honored as beautiful but silent moral examples, and they were encouraged to influence the morals of their nation as long as they did it in appropriate ways – perhaps by ministering to the sick in hospitals or by hosting teas to raise money for charitable causes. Yet Booth forcefully argued that women can and should be trained to preach and lead. They are not, she insisted, just decorations or silent influencers.

Booth wrote: "We cannot discover anything either unnatural or immodest in a Christian woman, becomingly attired, appearing on a platform or in a pulpit. By nature, she seems fitted to grace either. God has given to woman a graceful form and attitude, winning manners, persuasive speech, and, above all, a finely-toned emotional nature, all of which appear to us eminent natural qualifications for public speaking."

It is tragic that eloquent women preachers, such as Catherine Booth, had to defend their skills and anointing against clergy in the nineteenth century. It is even more tragic that equally anointed women preachers today must continue to defend themselves. When are we going to stop *quenching the Holy Spirit* by denying our sisters their right to prophesy? To keep them silent is to tune out the voice of the Spirit. To reject them is to reject the Lord's messengers.

We Must Not Hold Back the Righteousness that We Know to Tell

"For I am not ashamed of the gospel of Christ, for it is the power of God to salvation for everyone who believes, for the Jew first and also for the Greek. For in it the righteousness of God is revealed from faith to faith; as it is written, "The just shall live by faith." For the wrath of God is revealed from heaven against all ungodliness and unrighteousness of men, who suppress the truth in unrighteousness, because what may be known of God is manifest in them, for God has shown it to them. For since the creation of the world His invisible attributes are clearly seen, being understood by the things that are made, even His eternal power and Godhead, so that they are without excuse, because, although they knew God, they did not glorify Him as God, nor were thankful, but became futile in their thoughts, and their foolish hearts were darkened. Professing to be wise, they became fools, and changed the glory of the incorruptible God into an image made like corruptible man, and birds, and four-footed animals, and creeping things. Therefore, God also gave them up to uncleanness, in the lusts of their hearts, to dishonor their bodies among themselves, who exchanged the truth of God for a lie, and worshiped and served the creature rather than the Creator, who is blessed forever. Amen" (Romans 1:16-25 NKJV). *Selah*

    The apostle Paul, a servant of the Most-High God, wrote this epistle to the Romans. I see the apostle Paul as the preacher of preachers. No offense to the rest of the apostles, but Paul, in all his thirteen books, bears no shame of who he was (before conversion) or of Christ, whom he learned to love and share with others who were like him, in need of conversion, Amen. There were two things the Jews stumbled over or at: justification by faith without the works of the Law, and the admission of the Gentiles into the church, and therefore both these Paul studied to clear and vindicate.

In these two verses, 16 and 17, lies our proposition. The excellency of the gospel lies in this, *that it reveals to us (1) The salvation of believers as the end: It is the power of God unto salvation. Paul is not ashamed of the gospel, however mean and contemptible it may appear to a carnal eye, for the power of God works by it (the salvation). Salvation is like a map or guide to us who believe.

In this gospel, Paul talks about *the righteousness of God revealed.* Paul cuts through the chase, he searches the Word, convinces us of guilt and wrath, then shows us the way of salvation. This makes the gospel more welcome. We must first see the righteousness of God condemning, and then the righteousness of God justifying will appear worthy of all acceptance. In general, let's examine our focused verse, Romans 1:18, which describes the wrath of God, revealed against all ungodliness and unrighteousness of men, including those who explore scripture and what the Spirit says to them. The cause of their sinfulness is holding the truth in unrighteousness: that is, they knew (Jews, Gentiles, Protestants, and Christians alike) and professed them (righteousness and godliness) with their wicked courses. They held the truth as a captive, so that it would not influence them, for otherwise it would. An unrighteous, wicked heart is a place where many a good truth is detained and buried. Holding fast the form of sound words in faith and love is the root of all religion (2 Timothy 1:13), but holding it fast in unrighteousness is the root of all sin.

    Verse 18 continues to say, "The wrath of God is revealed from heaven not only in the written word, which is given by inspiration of God, but in the providences of God (divine direction). Wrath from heaven is revealed; it is not the wrath of a man like us, but wrath from heaven, therefore, the more terrible and the more unavoidable. Do not hold in your hearts something that God has given you to tell, by letter or mouth. If you don't tell what He has given you, you hold it with an ungodly and unrighteous heart. Even if it condemns you or tells on you, nevertheless, He will never harm you. He has manifested in you, as verse 19 shows, and has given it to you to spread. However, you are holding the gospel captive.

The Instructions Jesus Gave to All of Us

Luke 10: 1-3 (NKJV) says, "After these things, the Lord appointed seventy others also, and sent them two by two before His face into every city and place where He Himself was about to go. Then He said to them, 'The harvest truly is great, but the laborers are few; therefore, pray the Lord of the harvest to send out laborers into His harvest… Verse 3 continues, "Go your way; behold, I send you out as lambs among wolves;" not knowing that the wolves would be our pastors, and church clergy in sheep's clothing.

Moreover, anointed women of God, we must set out with prayer, and in prayer. We must look about, and see how great the harvest was, what abundance of people there were that wanted to have the gospel preached to them and were willing to receive it, nay, that had at this time their expectations raised of the coming of the Messiah and of His Kingdom.

NOTE: Anointed Women of God should apply themselves to their work under a deep concern for precious souls, looking upon them as the riches of this world, which ought to be secured for Christ. We must likewise be concerned that the *laborers* were so few.

The Jewish teachers were indeed many, but they were not *laborers;* they did not gather souls into God's Kingdom, but to their interest and party.

NOTE: Those who are good ministers themselves wish that there were more good ministers, for there is work for more. We must earnestly desire to receive their mission from God that *He* would send them forth as *laborers* into His harvest who is the Lord of the harvest, and that He would send others forth for, if God send them forth (the 72) they may hope He will go along with them and give them success. Let us therefore say, as the prophet (Isaiah 6:8), *Here I am, send me.* It is desirable to receive our commission from God, and then we may go on boldly. (Matthew Henry Commentary)

Respectively, receive "all" laborers of Christ. Do not hinder the Kingdom of God. The fairer offers we have of grace and life by Christ, the more we shall have to answer for another day, if we slight these offers: "It shall be more tolerable for Sodom than for that city (Luke 10:12)." The Sodomites indeed rejected the warning given them by Lot but rejecting the gospel (from God's mouthpiece) is a more heinous crime, and will be punished accordingly *in that day*. Jesus means the day of judgment (Luke 10:14), but calls it, by way of emphasis, *that day*, because it is the last and great day, the day when we must account for all the days of time, and have our state determined for the *days of eternity*.

Her Story

Equally important is the role of female clergy in modern American society, spanning the 20th and 21st centuries. Barbara J. MacHaffie, *Her Story*, 2nd ed., breaks it down in agenda status for clarity. Denominational reports and special studies were important vehicles for this self-discovery and new consciousness. An American Baptist report in 1968, for example, revealed only a small percentage of women on the church's national staff. Most of these women occupied low-level posts as administrative assistants. The number of women in upper-level jobs had actually decreased between 1958 and 1968. A year later, a special report to the General Assembly of the United Presbyterian Church acknowledged that a "profound bias" against women continued to exist in the Christian community. A similar statistical study in the United Methodist Church documented the inferior status and limited roles of women, showing, among other things, that fewer than 1 percent of active, ordained Methodist ministers were women.

Another vehicle that acquainted women with the realities of inequality was the vast body of literature that emerged during the early 1970s on sexism in the churches. Some of this material simply described ecclesiastical inequality, observing that women were finding more opportunities for participation and dignity outside rather than inside the Christian community. Other publications tried to analyze the causes of sexual inequality in the churches by probing history and the biased ways in which the biblical material had been interpreted. These publications made women aware that they were confronting images and roles that were deeply rooted in the Judeo-Christian tradition.

Women in many denominations also became conscious of their situation through formal and informal discussions with other women. From seminary lounges to church Bible study groups to preplanned gatherings, such as the World Council of Churches' Conference on Sexism in 1974, women began to share both positive and negative experiences of living and working in the Christian tradition. Like much of the literature on women, the groups were frequently ecumenical. This kind of communal experience provided some women with a chance to talk about their frustrations, learn that they were not alone, and make a start at building relationships with other women. These group gatherings would eventually provide a new setting for theology in the Christian community.

Black women as a group also began to examine their status in the Christian communities. For centuries, they operated as the glue that held the Black community together, reflecting their African heritage of economic and religious importance. In the face of profound oppression, they cared about preserving and continuing prayer, education, family life, and the programs of the churches. Yet they realized that they had been systematically excluded from positions of authority and leadership. In Black Methodism, for example, women were deaconesses and even influential preachers but had no official place in power structures dominated by men. Rosemary Radford Ruether observes that the Black church has been "super patriarchal" because only in the church did the Black man find an opportunity for power, which was denied to him in society at large. Black women may have acquiesced in this because they recognized the degradation that White society inflicted on men of color. Eventually, however, women also began to resent the fact that their strength was regarded with humiliation by Black men and their experiences were ignored by Black theologians.

The outcome of these exercises in self-discovery and awareness was the formation of more permanent organizations within ecclesiastical structures to seek justice for women. The American Baptist Convention, for example, formed its Executive Staff Women in 1969 to study the involvement of women in the churches and then followed this up with a task force on women. A United Methodist Women's Caucus was established to promote the rights and participation of women within that denomination. In 1973, the Presbyterians organized their Council on Women and the Church to identify issues relevant to the status of women in the church and society.

Due in part to changes in the status of women in American culture, the advocacy of such church organizations and the entry of growing numbers of women into seminaries and the clergy, the last quarter of the twentieth century was a period of change for men and women in the Christian community. Significant numbers of women have begun to appear on church governing bodies and in the ordained ministry. For some of them, breaking institutional barriers and settling into the existing church is sufficient. But others have seen themselves as agents of transformation in both radical and moderate forms. They are attempting to construct a different theology and a different style of ministry, arguing that women will only truly experience inclusion when change comes in how the Christian faith is organized and symbolized. Some of this transformation is spontaneous and unconscious, some is carefully planned and executed. Some women, such as feminist interpreters of the Bible, have had a significant impact, while the ultimate effect of feminist influence in areas such as worship is less certain.

PART 2: PATTERNS OF THE FATHER

Chapter 6

ANOINTED WOMEN OF GOD…WE ARE GOD'S PARADIGM!

WOMEN OF GOD…We will forever be recognized as a 'paradigm' changer! "Paradigm" simply means "pattern," from the Greek word *paradeigma*.

Vashti Murphy McKenzie

This woman is the first female consecrated and elected bishop of the African Methodist Episcopal denomination, highlighting the significance of the term 'paradigm.' Bishop McKenzie says, The pattern contains the attitudes, thoughts, and behaviors that make up a person's lifestyle. Like the pattern used to cut pieces of cloth for a garment, the pattern defines the boundaries of the pieces and indicates how to assemble them successfully; it constitutes the rules and regulations for sewing the garment. To change the garment or accommodate changes in the wearer, such as size, weight, or height, a new pattern must be made.

The paradigm, or pattern, in the cultural societal sense, therefore, is the blueprint for how a person assembles the pieces of their life. Changes in a person's life exert pressure on the pattern. The pattern can either shift to adapt to a new reality or remain stationary, inhibiting change.

For many centuries, the pattern from which the garment of pastoral leadership was constructed did not include any pieces that allowed clergywomen to be sewn into the prophetic leadership fabric of congregational life. The pattern is not a new one: Its structure was drawn from the holy writ, was distorted by sexism, and reemerges as a new idea (Joel 2:28, Acts 2:17, and Gal. 3:27-28).

History reflects many female paradigm busters. The role of women breaking into traditionally male-dominated fields, such as business, politics, sports, and religion, is not a new story. Some of the women who have effectively stormed the heights of exclusionary social paradigms include Madame C. J. Walker, entrepreneur; Shirley Chisholm, presidential candidate; Mary McCloud Bethune, presidential adviser; Carol Mosely Braun, U. S. senator; Rev. Pauli Murray, first Episcopal priest; Bishop Leontyne Kelly, retired United Methodist episcopate; Lena Horne, entertainer; Oprah Winfrey, entertainment entrepreneur. However, they did not achieve their accomplishments without struggle.

The new story is the fact that women are bringing pressure to bear on all-male paradigms in such great numbers. Notably, women are not only redesigning the pattern but are also surviving and succeeding. The impact of millions of women competing in the same job market for the same jobs (including pulpits, appointments, denominational roles, and tenure in seminaries) exerts a tremendous impact on the tapestry of religious life. Millions of women worldwide are challenging existing power patterns, infusing them with more humanistic values. The influx of women in leadership positions in the church and church-related professions is on the rise. Women are serving as bishops, presiding elders, district superintendents, pastors, elders, deacons, chaplains, pastoral counselors, campus ministers, seminary professors, and denominational officers. (*Not Without A Struggle: Leadership Development for African American women in Ministry*, Vashti Murphy McKenzie, 1996.)

A "Well" Pattern of Defining Moments
John 4: 3-26 (NKJV)

"Jesus left Judea and departed again to Galilee. But he needed to go through Samaria. So, He came to a city in Samaria, which is called Sychar, near the plot of ground that Jacob had given to his son Joseph. Now Jacob's well was there. Jesus, therefore, being wearied from His journey, sat thus by the well. It was about the sixth hour. A woman of Samaria came to draw water. Jesus said to her, 'Give me a drink.' For His disciples had gone away into the city to buy food. Then the woman of Samaria said to Him, 'How is it that You, being a Jew, ask a drink from me, a Samaritan woman? For Jews have no dealings with Samaritans.' Jesus answered and said to her, 'If you knew the gift of God, and who it is who says to you, 'Give Me a drink,' you would have asked Him, and He would have given you living water.' The woman said to Him, 'Sir, You have nothing to draw with, and the well is deep. Where then do You get that living water? 'Are You greater than our father Jacob, who gave us the well, and drank from it himself, as well as his sons and his livestock?' Jesus answered and said to her, Whoever drinks of this water will thirst again, 'but whoever drinks of the water that I shall give him will never thirst. But the water that I shall give him will become in him a fountain of water springing up into everlasting life.' The woman said to Him, 'Sir, give me this water, that I may not thirst, nor come here to draw.' Jesus said to her, 'Go, call your husband, and come here.' The woman answered and said, 'I have no husband.' Jesus said to her, 'You have well said, I have no husband, for you have had five husbands, and the one whom you now have is not your husband; in that you spoke truly.' The woman said to Him, 'Sir, I perceive that You are a prophet. Our fathers worshiped on this mountain, and you Jews say that in Jerusalem is the place where one ought to worship.' Jesus said to her, 'Woman, believe Me, the hour is coming when you will neither on this mountain, nor in Jerusalem, worship the Father. You worship what you do not know; we know what we worship, for salvation is of the Jews. But the hour is coming, and now is, when the true worshipers will worship the Father in spirit and truth; for the Father is seeking such to worship Him. God is Spirit, and those who worship Him must worship in spirit and truth.' The woman said to Him, 'I know that the Messiah is coming' (who is called Christ). When He comes, He will tell us all things.' Jesus said to her, 'I who speak to you am He.'"

In addition, Lisa Sergio defines it in an exciting discovery of what he offered her. Thus, sitting alongside a well in the quiet countryside of Samaria, an alien land, Jesus was laying down a great verity, not to His disciples or learned men, but to a very simple Samaritan woman who was living in sin. Why? Merely to touch or redeem one woman who was not even of His own people? No, not merely to reach one woman but to speak to all women, however exalted or humble, rich, or poor, bright, or dull of mind, virtuous or sinful, women of that day or any day.

Then Jesus fell silent, and the words he had spoken began to take on their true significance in the woman's mind. As though a ray of unexpected light had penetrated her obtuseness, making her understand the nature of what he was saying, she told him: "I know that Messiah is coming, and when he comes, he will tell us everything." Presently, from the Nazarene's lips, with dramatic simplicity, came the revelation: "I am he. I, who am speaking to you now." Never before had he been willing to answer the question, 'Who are you?' so frequently asked of him by friends and foes alike. It was a woman who had not asked it, who received the fateful answer: He was the Messiah.

The Samaritan looked at him in silence, and for a brief moment, time seemed to stand still, absorbing the sound of His words. A translucent sky, a valley basking in the sun, a backdrop of hills stately in their robes of light and shadow, had become witness to the unique encounter between a prophet sent by God and a simple woman who, in her namelessness, represented all womankind. Sinful as she was, suspicious as she had been, and overly concerned with trivial matters, unable at first to comprehend what she had heard, the Samaritan was suddenly awake to a new and startling reality. However, the barriers of prejudice that Jesus and the woman had reduced to shatters seemed present only as the broken pieces of some object, now despised and useless. (*Jesus and Woman*: An exciting discovery of what he offered her, Lisa Sergio)

The Samaritan woman had a defining moment at the well when she faced herself and the Son of God. She realized that she was a woman of value and worth and that her past was not held against her. She now had something powerful to share. She immediately ran back to her village and convinced the community to return with her to the well to meet this man Jesus, who had told her everything she had ever done. This pass-around woman with a tainted lifestyle not only knew who the Messiah was but chatted with Him at the well. The Divine was present in her situation. Things had not changed; she had. He was present in her circumstances, and we all want the Divine to be present in the time of trouble. If He doesn't change our lives, He will change us to handle our lives. This desert dweller had to be someone very special, for Christ would not spend precious moments on the unimportant people in important times.

Jesus validated her, and her stock in the community rose considerably that day. She was compelled to share the good news; her revelation must have been dramatic because the same people who had gossiped and looked down on her before now came to the well with her, in the heat of the day, to see and hear this Jesus for themselves. The woman at the well had found purpose in life beyond mere survival. (*Journey to the Well*, Vashti Murphy McKenzie)

A "Resurrected" Pattern of Defining Moments
Luke 24:1-11(NKJV)

Defining moments to go and tell…At Jesus' resurrection, the women found themselves on the telling end of this narrative. Scripture reads, "Now on the first *day* of the week, very early in the morning, they, and *certain other women* with them, came to the tomb bringing the spices which they had prepared. But they found the stone rolled away from the tomb. Then they went in and did not find the body of the Lord Jesus. And it happened, as they were greatly perplexed about this, that behold, two men stood by them in shining garments. Then, as they were afraid and bowed their faces to the earth, they said to them, 'Why do you seek the living among the dead? He is not here, but is risen! Remember how He spoke to you when He was still in Galilee, saying, the Son of Man must be delivered into the hands of sinful men, and be crucified, and the third day rise again.' And they remembered His words. Then they returned from the tomb and told all these things to the eleven and to all the rest. It was Mary Magdalene, Joanna, Mary *the mother* of James, and the other *women* with them, who told these things to the apostles. And their words seemed to them like idle tales, and they did not believe them."

    Similarly, the apostles of Jesus' day did not believe the women; the same holds true for male clergy today. Men from all cultures are still doubting our story, labeling us as crazy, and that we should be kitchen-bound. But there is a story to tell! And God's women are going to speak with boldness! Speaking about Jesus and His attributes is like finding treasure that was only meant for you to find. When Jesus speaks, all who are called and appointed will answer.

At the resurrection tomb. The sun had not yet risen in the sky, and not a person was out on the road. As Mary alternately ran and walked, her breath short less from exertion than from astonishment, all that had happened in the previous thirty-six hours came back to her as clearly as if she were living it for the first time. She realized that the tiny band of heartbroken followers of the Nazarene who had remained as near as they could be to the foot of the cross had consisted of four women and only one man–John, the Nazarene's youngest and dearest disciple. The women had been Mary, mother of Jesus, Salome, mother of John, Mary, mother of James and Joseph, and she, Mary of Magdala. She knew that Peter, the disciple who had not fled as did all the others when Jesus was apprehended in the Garden of Gethsemane, was now somewhere in seclusion, burning with remorse for his threefold denial. Nine of the eleven were hiding in fear. John on Golgotha with the women was concerned with Mary of Nazareth, who had refused to abandon the small corner of stony ground on which she sat as near the cross as she was allowed. Huddling together, the other three women had suppressed any display of grief lest the guards, who wanted no problems, force them into silence or remove them from the hill; every second of his agony had also been their agony. But she, Mary of Magdala, loved him with a pervading ardor, and her despair had been almost beyond endurance as she helplessly watched him die. Yet she had not flinched, her tragic eyes riveted on the bleeding face until the end.

Nevertheless, at the tomb, while looking into the tomb, Mary Magdalene saw two figures in white sitting, one at the head and one at the foot of the niche where the body had lain. They had not been there when John and Peter had visited the place only minutes before. One of the white-clad figures, seeing the tears in her eyes, had asked her solicitously why she was crying. She had answered: 'They have taken my Lord away and I do not know where they have laid him.' As she was about to turn around to leave the tomb, a voice, not very distinct because it was outside, asked the same question: 'Why are you weeping?' Stepping out and thinking the questioner was a gardener, she said: 'If it is you, sir, who removed him, tell me where you have laid him and I will take him away.'

It was then that the unmistakable voice called her name: 'Mary!' and she recognized Jesus standing within reach of her hand! As she tried to touch him, he interrupted her gesture, then he bade her take a message to the disciples.

Even as she hurried to fulfill his command, the vision of Jesus was still before her eyes, his person as real as he had ever been in life! Quickly, she blurted out to the men: 'I have seen the Lord! I have seen the Lord!' and gave them his message. Her shattering experience bore witness to one of the most moving and beautiful episodes in the Gospel, even as it was the first announcement of what was to become a central fact of Christian faith: Jesus had risen from the dead!"

It cannot have been mere happenstance that the bearing of this crucial message–the announcement of the Master's resurrection–fell to the lot of a woman. No more than it had been happenstance that the woman of Samaria was sent to tell her men that the Jew who had spoken to her at Jacob's Well was the long-awaited Messiah. It is not reasonable to ignore the fact that the two great cornerstones of Christian faith (Jesus of Nazareth is the Messiah and He rose again from the dead) were each first revealed to a woman who, as the

Nazarene's appointed messenger, was sent to disclose it to her men. The Samaritan woman, a stranger to Jesus and inimical to his people, was sent to convey the news among strangers. Mary of Magdala, one of the Master's most faithful followers, a woman of his own race and a native of his region, was sent to convey the news to his intimates. Thus, it was by the word of a woman that tidings so fundamental in Christianity were made known to persons representing the two extremes of a spectrum of local relationships, symbolic of relationships in the world as a whole: the enemies and the friends.

Truly, there is a need for women such as she, Mary of Magdala, in today's world. Women who can bring out of their depths the activism, the meditative, and the mysticism, the seeds of which are dormant in every human being. But when Jesus sent the Magdalene, as he had once sent the Samaritan, to be his messenger to men, he was making it unmistakably clear that humankind is a partnership and that sharing is its lifeline. Whatever Jesus gave to woman, be it confirmation of his mission expressed by the word Messiah, be it the revelation of a portent such as his return from the dead, the gift was not for her alone. It was for all mankind, of which she represented only half. Her duty was to share it with the men and to make it acceptable by virtue of her understanding of its value. The men's part was then to carry the gift further by their particular power of outreach, by their particular activism, and their particular spiritual drive. (Sergio 104-05).

A "Catholic Visionary" Pattern of Defining Moments

Formerly, the enthusiasm for visionary women in general and the immensely talented polymath Hildegard of Bingen in particular raises disturbing interpretative questions. For Hildegard is in no way typical, either as a nun or as a visionary or as a female writer. As Professor Newman notes in her introduction, Hildegard was profoundly different from later figures such as Catherine of Siena and Teresa of Avila, the only women taken seriously as theologians or mystics by the Catholic Church, until recently. Nor is Hildegard, who is, in any case, a complicated writer, made easier to understand by isolating her from her twelfth-century German monastic context and relocating her in a tradition of female spirituality that runs from Perpetua (d. 203) to Therese of Lisieux (d. 1897). A Benedictine abbess, Hildegard advocated a monastic life of obedience and communal prayer, not the extravagant and individualistic asceticism of some later medieval women. A proponent of Gregorian reform, Hildegard proselytized for clerical purity and power, and argued that women should not hold priestly office, although she (virtually alone among medieval women) undertook preaching missions with ecclesiastical approval. Authorized to write by God's command (as were many other medieval women), Hildegard dominated her confessors, scribes, and illustrators in a way not common with female saints, some of whom (such as Elizabeth of Hungary or Angela of Foligno) were so controlled by their confessor-scribes that it is indeed hard to know whether their piety and even their words represent truly the divine message they heard in the inner recesses of their hearts.

Moreover, Hildegard was a prophetic seer whose visions had political content and were based on a physical experience of light and pain. She wrote in Old Testament images of precious stones and noble buildings, of agriculture and organic growth, of courts and war, and of beautiful garments–images radically different from the more tender, domestic, and even sentimental meditations on the holy family and the human experience of Jesus common in Rhineland convents of the fourteenth century. A visionary who took her revelations as a text for exegesis, not an experience for re-living, Hildegard was not, technically speaking, a mystic at all. She wrote not about union but about doctrine, although her attention to bodily phenomena such as sexual desire or menstrual cramps sets her apart from other visionary theologians of the twelfth century (such as Hugh or Richard of St. Victor).

Readers who come to the complex and difficult text presented here equipped with a background in feminist theology or women's history may be surprised by many things, among them Hildegard's sense of inferiority as a female and her confident self-assertion in castigating the clergy. The flood of questions raised by recent work on women's piety needs to be addressed, if only by spelling out clearly two issues at stake. First, is there a female spirituality in the period between 1100 and 1517? Second, did medieval women speak with their voices and out of their own experience, or is their work merely the inscription of the misogynist and patriarchal values of the dominant religious tradition? Although related, these are not the same question.

To ask the first question is really to ask whether there are consistent and identifiable ways in which women's religious concerns, considered across decades, classes, and national or linguistic lines, differ from those of men. The question does not, as some have argued, make essentialist assumptions about the "eternal feminine." To be sure, there were biological constraints affecting women's roles in the medieval period – constraints of which Hildegard, with her keen medical curiosity, was well aware. But no modern theorist would explain women's religious options or opinions as biologically determined. There were, however, institutional and educational constraints not rooted in biology that were constant throughout the later Middle Ages. Women were prohibited from holding priestly office and increasingly from exercising roles as preachers and spiritual counselors. They were cut off from the new scholastic education of the twelfth and thirteenth centuries. Yet, they found encouragement and opportunities to write when vernacular languages and genres emerged during the much-studied shift from oral to written culture. The question of women's piety is, therefore, in part a question of whether social, educational, and institutional limitations were so powerful an influence as to fundamentally differentiate women's insights from those of men.

The second question asked in recent decades about women's writing is also complex. Both radical feminists and conservative students of mysticism have queried whether what we have in women's texts from the twelfth to the fifteenth century are women's voices at all. In a culture where official theology was defined by scholastic debate and papal pronouncement, where reception of the eucharist required the recipient to submit to previous scrutiny by a male confessor, where increasingly elaborate rules were devised for *testing* charismatic gifts, which could be adjudged *feigned sanctity*, how can we be sure we hear women speaking freely? Can phrases such as Hildegard's repeated assertion of female inferiority be accepted as women's own, even when penned or dictated by the woman herself?

Some scholars have wished to decide this issue a priori, declaring women's writing either a vague echo of more theoretically powerful works by orthodox males or a species of *false consciousness* that reflects merely patriarchal repression. This position assumes not only that women's courage, serenity, self-sacrifice, and loyalty were self-delusion but also that the power to repress is the only effective power in human history. To this a priori assumption, scholarly scrutiny of texts can, of course, provide no rebuttal. However, recent scholarship not committed to this ideological position has found in Hildegard, as in Catherine of Siena, Julian of Norwich, or even (for all their orientation toward male advisers – Elizabeth of

Schönau or Dorothy of Montau) the welling up of profound female experience. The low-key irony with which Hildegard reminded corrupt clerics that God had been forced to choose an inferior mouthpiece because they had fallen so low, and the cheeky casuistry with which the fourteenth-century Englishwoman Margery Kempe met the admonition not to preach, have hardly seemed to recent interpreters to be an internalization of misogyny. Nor have all scholars read as repression Hildegard's glorious sense of the power and independence conferred on women by virginity.

It would, however, be misleading to close with general methodological issues raised by the current discussion of female spirituality. Attentive readers will find that Hildegard directs her audience not to a consideration of women but to a consideration of humankind. (HILDEGARD OF BINGEN - SCIVIAS 1990).

Chapter 7

JESUS And WOMEN: What Did Jesus Do?

Subsequently, the 21st-century writer and author Joe E. Trull, a professor in Christian ethics, introduces an article that boldly and transparently addresses the stance Jesus took regarding women. In this century, fundamental equality for women has finally been realized. A dramatic reversal also has occurred in society's attitude toward the mistreatment of females. However, many voices are crying for greater liberation and justice for women.

Where Does the Church Stand in All Of This?

Many accuse the Christian community of supporting beliefs and practices that perpetuate female subordination. Is it possible that the church of Jesus Christ may have defended social customs rather than upheld God's ideal in gender relationships? Does the example of Jesus provide guidelines?

To interpret Jesus' treatment of women in the first century correctly, an understanding of the New Testament world is absolutely essential. Although Jewish women occupied a position of dignity and responsibility in the home, in social life, they were little more than an appendage of their husbands.

In William Barclay's book, *The Letters to Timothy, Titus and Philemon*, he noted, "In Jewish law, she was not a person but a thing; she was entirely at the disposal of her father or of her husband. She was forbidden to learn the law; to instruct a woman in the law was to cast pearls before swine." Jewish women who were not allowed any part in the synagogue service, could not teach in school, and their testimony was not credible evidence in court.

In the Graeco-Roman world, the situation was no better. The respectable Greek woman lived a secluded life, confined to her quarters. Usually, the wife appeared in public only once or twice each year, usually during religious festivals or at a relative's funeral. The reason for the wife's seclusion was her primary role in the marriage: to bear a male heir for her husband. Demosthenes explained the accepted rule of life: "We have courtesans for the sake of pleasure; we have concubines for the sake of daily cohabitation; we have wives for the purpose of having children legitimately, and of having a faithful guardian of all our houschold affairs" (Barclay, *The Letters to the Galatians and Ephesians*).

In stark contrast to this universal denigration of first-century females, Jesus' attitude toward women was totally countercultural. Sweeping aside centuries of tradition and prejudice, Jesus' treatment of women was revolutionary. What did he do? Christ simply related to women in the same way he related to men, never regarding females as inferior in any way.

Four biblical examples illustrate the contrast. In the encounter with the woman at the well, Jesus recognized women as persons capable of responding to God (John 4:7-30). No rabbi would have spoken to any woman in public, especially this Samaritan with a sinful past.

The First Person to Whom Jesus revealed
Himself as God's Messiah
Was a Foreign Female

In Jesus' day, the double standard prevailed. Men could commit adultery with little consequence, but guilty women often were stoned. To the group about to execute a woman caught "in the very act of committing adultery" (John 8:4), Jesus clearly condemned this censorious spirit and double standard (John 8:7).

Another episode occurred in the home of Martha and her sister, Mary, where Jesus confronted stereotyped female roles (Luke 10:38-42). Martha was upset with Mary not just because she was shirking her duties, but also because she was "out of her place." Mary dared to relate to Jesus as only men were allowed, listening and learning about God. Jesus not only defended her right to do so but also seemed to invite Martha to join her.

A final episode occurred on the first Easter morning. In ancient Judaism, only the witness of two or more men was admissible evidence in court. Yet all four Gospels record that the first witnesses to the empty tomb were women (John 20:1-18).

By Announcing the Resurrection Through the Testimony of Women,
God Affirmed Their Role in Sharing the Good News.

What do these biblical examples mean? Simply this: Jesus refused to reinforce the cultural misunderstandings of his day about the status of women. Jesus never suggested that women are weak or easily deceived. Nor does he forbid women to study the Scriptures or teach his Word. Rather,

Jesus intentionally treated all daughters of Eve as persons created in God's image, responsible to God for their lives and the use of their gifts.

The New Testament church followed Jesus' example. Pentecost was Emancipation Day as God's Spirit was equally poured out on men and women (Acts 2:17-18). As the Christian faith spread throughout the civilized world, the strategic role of women became evident. Churches were founded in the homes of women, such as Lydia of Philippi (Acts 16:14-15). Women emerged as church leaders in Thessalonica (Acts 17:4), Berea (Acts 17:12), Athens (Acts 17:34), and Corinth (Acts 18:1-8). Paul named eleven women in his list of prominent leaders in the church at Rome, including Phoebe, a "servant" in the church (Romans 16:1-2).

In a day when women were severely restricted from participating in social life. It is remarkable that Christian women played a significant role in the early church. In fact, this change in women's roles in the New Testament churches precipitated much discussion about females in Paul's letters (1 Corinthians 11:2-16, 14:33-36; Ephesians 5:26-33; 1 Timothy 2:11-15, 3:1-13).

Most importantly, as God's ultimate revelation, Jesus' treatment of women was determinative. What did Jesus do? Simply this. In a day when women were universally subjugated, denigrated, and mistreated, Jesus affirmed females as persons created in God's image, equal in worth and equal in responsibility to God (Genesis 1:26-27). Jesus liberated women from slavery to sin and from demeaning social customs, inviting them to work, witness, and serve Christ in the church and the world (Luke 8:13).

Satan Attacks God

Meanwhile, Satan is blocking the thoughts of mankind as anointed women of God push to spread the gospel of Jesus Christ. In *The Invisible War*,

Ingram states that Satan is a master counterfeiter. His attacks against the work that God does in this world are often indirect. He crafts attractive alternatives to the gospel and the church, many of which contain a lot of truth but with just enough error to corrupt the entire system. If he can get non-Christians to sincerely believe in a seemingly noble cause, a false belief system, or a charitable work, he can convince them that they don't need the gospel at all. If he can get Christians to mix some of his deceptions into their faith, he can fool us into living according to the world even while we are convinced that we are living according to the gospel. The subtleties of his schemes produce a vast selection of counterfeits to the real thing.

The New Testament spells out some of these attacks for us. Colossians 2:8 informs us that Satan takes people captive through false philosophies. In 1 Corinthians 10:20, he is exposed as the mastermind behind false religions. He inspires many people within his domain to pose as ministers.

These false servants then lead people astray as they mix and mingle with true servants of God (2 Corinthians 11:14-15). Satan is also the source of false doctrine through the teachings of many antichrists (1 John 2:18). Jesus told a parable in Matthew 13:24-30 in which Satan makes counterfeit disciples and scatters them among the real ones, *those disciples who welcome all of God's anointed to share in the spreading of His gospel.* False morals may seem like the product only of human ignorance to us, but 2 Thessalonians 2:7-12 attributes them to the work of the deceiver. According to the Bible, the source of all falsehood, all misguided worldviews, all counterfeit religions and philosophies, and all teachers of any belief other than faith in the gospel of Jesus Christ are instigated, inspired, and influenced by the father of lies.

This Is a Man's World?

"This is a man's world, this is a man's world

But it wouldn't be nothing, nothing

Without a woman or a girl."

Do not take this song literally or think James Brown wrote it; in fact, he didn't write the song. The lyrics were written by a woman inspired by the Bible. Betty Jean Newsome was a former girlfriend of Brown's, whom he had met at the famous Apollo Theater in Harlem. Newsome was inspired to write the lyrics after reading Genesis 2, in which God creates Eve out of Adam's rib. To Newsome, "It's a Man's, Man's, Man's World" is actually a gospel song, a meditation on the Lord's design. As she told *The Village Voice in 2007*: "I was just reading the Bible and thinking about how wonderful and powerful man is …God, He can create, He can take man's rib out of his body and make a woman. I was just sitting there and thinking about how, after all of these things that He made and He did, all of it was worthless without a woman, and you gotta have those kids, or a girl. That's where the girl part comes in."

Newsome's lyrics pack in a lot of truth. It is a bald fact that the majority of our material and institutional culture comes to us because of the work and creativity of men. Take the technology of the past 600 years: the printing press, the refrigerator, the lightbulb, the automobile, the phone, and the computer are all things that we can't imagine living without, which were invented by men. The great philosophers, thinkers, and teachers were men, by and large, as were the great political rulers; nations rose and fell because of the rule of men. The number of women who have contributed to these fields is, by comparison, so small that they are typically listed in women's history books. (See, when men do things, it's "history," but when women do things, it's special "feminine history.")

Of course, the situation has improved in the relatively recent past. Women today contribute enormously to the global economy. In most developing nations, women play a crucial role in sustaining financial growth and supporting their families and communities. In the West, it is now widely accepted that women should have the opportunity to pursue education, and an increasing number of leaders and politicians in developing countries are embracing this principle as well. Within the church, women are teaching the Bible, evangelizing the nations, and leading nonprofits.

And, to return to Newsome's lyrics, men would be "nothing without a woman or a girl." Even if women appear only rarely in the history books, none of us would exist without women. Men can make bridges and books and bombs, but they can't make babies. And beyond their biological role, women in every time and place have "made something of the world," even if they were typically seen as bit players in men's stories rather than main players in their own.

But the phrase 'This Is a Man's World' is true in another way: It accurately reflects a broken world, a world as it should *not* be. God never intended for men to reign over creation alone. He made all image bearers, men and women, who together reflect the image of God, to be His representatives on earth, to reign and rule over both material and institutional culture (Gen. 1:28). It might be a man's world. Still, it was supposed to be a world governed by men *and* women. And in societies like ours, where the locus of cultural influence is the marketplace (and no longer the home), women must be *in* the marketplace in order to shape material and institutional culture.

When Psalm 8 calls to exercise dominion falls more or less to only half the human population, then the creation and fellow humans fail to flourish (*A Woman's Place*, K. Beaty).

PART 3: PROBLEM FORMATION

Chapter 8
PROBLEM FORMATION

In this situation, how can we solve the problem of male clergy dishonoring God's anointed female clergy? Can we treat them the way that they treat us? No. Can we simply bow down to man and distance ourselves, as clergywomen, from the call of God? No. How can we receive the 'help meet' partnership that God gave to both man and woman from Eden's paradise once again?

First and foremost, we go to the light. King David says in Psalm 27:1-14, "The LORD is our light and our salvation; Whom shall we fear? The LORD is the strength of our life; Of whom shall we be afraid? When the wicked came against us, to eat up our flesh, our enemies and foes, they stumbled and fell. Though an army may encamp against us, our heart shall not fear; Though war may rise against us, in this we will be confident. One thing we have desired of the LORD, That I will seek; That we may dwell in the house of the LORD All the days of our lives, To behold the beauty of the LORD, And to inquire in His temple. For in the time of trouble He shall hide us in His pavilion; In the secret place of His tabernacle, He shall hide us; He shall set us high upon a rock. And now our head shall be lifted above our enemies all around us; Therefore, we will offer sacrifices of joy in His tabernacle; We will sing, yes, we will sing praises to the LORD. Hear, O LORD, when we cry with our voices! Have mercy also upon us, and answer us. When You said, "Seek My face," Our heart said to You, "Your face, LORD, we will seek." Do not hide Your face from us; Do not turn Your servants away in anger; You have been our help; Do not leave us nor forsake us, O god of our salvation. When our father and our mother forsake us, then the LORD will take care of us. Teach us Your way, O LORD, And lead us in a smooth path, because of our enemies. Do not deliver us to the will of our adversaries; For false witnesses have risen against us, And such as breathed out violence. We would have lost heart. Unless we had believed That we would see the goodness of the LORD in the land of the living. Wait on the LORD; Be of good courage, And He shall strengthen our heart; Wait, We say, on the LORD!"

To begin with, what made this a problem, and how can it be resolved? It is a fact that men's attack on female clergy has become habitual in repetitive ways, as if discussed in a private room that only a group of men can attend, for the direction of division. Eyewitnesses have experienced man's handiwork from male clergy who:

- Speak amongst themselves to ouster any woman of God from approaching the sacred altar, from preaching the gospel of Christ

- Not acknowledging any female clergy of God who sits in God's house
- Not offering a place of solitude for preparation to speak to congregations of Christ
- When the female speaker is asked to come into a pastor's office before service, all male clergy leave, leaving the female clergy alone in the pastor's study. A pastor's study, meant for spiritual meditation, has become full of worldly spirits and is allowed by pastors.
- Not allowing female clergy to sit in or preach from the sacred pulpit, but at the bottom of the sacred area on the floor, at a lectern in the middle of the church. Using God's Scripture, 1 Timothy 2:11-15 [it is really 2:12 alone in all the Bible that bears the weight of the opposition to women in ministry and leadership]. "Right off the bat, the tone here doesn't sound like the Paul who is so positive toward all the women in Romans 16. It doesn't sound like the Paul who gently urges Euodia and Syntyche to get along–

they are co-laborers. If you know Paul's writings and the story of Acts thoroughly, your first thought is, "Something's going on here." (A Biblical Argument for Women in Ministry and Leadership, Ken Schenck)

In other words, we need the **assistance** of Watzlawick, Weakland, Fisch, and Erickson, as outlined in *Change: Principles of Problem Formation and Problem Resolution* (1974). These Christian brothers have, in their extremely important book, looked at this phenomenon of change and put it into a conceptual framework illuminated by examples from a variety of areas. It opens up new pathways to the further understanding of how people become enmeshed in problems with each other, and new pathways to expediting the resolution of such human impasses. The relevance of this new framework extends far beyond the sphere of 'psychological' problems from which it grew. Their work is fascinating. For this reason, Erickson and I think that it is a noteworthy contribution and a must for anyone seeking to understand the various aspects of group behavior. In this instance, our problem, male clergy's refusal to share in God's plan with their counterpart, women of Christ, is deceitful. Satan has put a blindfold on their minds.

Subsequently, while many theories of persistence and change have been formulated throughout the centuries of Western culture, these have primarily been theories of persistence or theories of change, rather than theories of persistence *and* change. That is, the tendency has been either to view persistence and invariance as a "natural" or "spontaneous" state, to be taken for granted and needing no explanation, and change as the problem to be explained, or to take the inverse position. The very fact that either position can be adopted so readily suggests that they are complementary, and what is problematic is not absolute and somehow inherent in the nature of things, but depends on the particular case and point of view involved. Such a concept is consistent with our experience of human affairs and the difficulties they present. For example, whenever we observe a person, a family, or a wider social system enmeshed in a problem persistently and repetitively, despite desire and effort to alter the situation, *two* questions arise equally: "How does this undesirable situation persist?" and "What is required to change it?"

In the course of their work, they have made some progress not only toward answering these questions in particular cases but also toward developing a broader view. Rather than retracing this long road, however, they feel that two abstract and general theories, drawn from the field of mathematical logic, may be utilized to help present and clarify some of the conclusions at which we have arrived. These are 1) The Theory of Groups and 2) the Theory of Logical Types. *In doing so, they are fully aware that their use of these theories is far from satisfying mathematical rigor. It should be taken as an attempt at exemplification through analogy.*

Namely, in this case, we will examine the Theory of Logical Types to help address our issue of who can spread the Gospel of Christ, specifically about gender roles. However, what Group Theory apparently cannot provide is a model for those types of change that transcend a given system or frame of reference. At this point, we must turn to the Theory of Logical Types. This theory, too, begins with the concept of collections of "things" which are united by a specific characteristic common to all of them. As in Group Therapy, the components of the totality are called *members*, while the totality itself is called *a class rather than a* group. One essential rule of the Theory of Logical Types is that "whatever involves *all* of a collection must not be one of the collections," as Whitehead and Russell state it in their monumental work *Principia Mathematica* (101). It should be immediately obvious that mankind is the class of all individuals, but that it is not itself an individual. Any attempt to deal with the one in terms of the other is doomed to lead to nonsense and confusion. For example, the economic behavior of the population of a large city cannot be understood in terms of the behavior of one inhabitant multiplied by, say, four million. This, incidentally, was precisely the mistake committed in the early days of economic theory and is now scornfully referred to as the Robinson Crusoe economic model. A population of four million is not just quantitatively but qualitatively different from an individual, because it involves systems of interaction among the individuals. Similarly, while the individual members of a species are usually endowed with very specific survival mechanisms, it is well known that the entire species may race headlong towards extinction, and the human species is probably no exception.

Conversely, in totalitarian ideologies the individual is seen only as a member of a class and thus becomes unimportant and expendable, an ant in an anthill, or as Koestler has so aptly put it regarding his fellow inmate Nicolas in the death row of a Spanish prison: "In this view Nicolas existed merely as a social abstraction, a mathematical unit, obtained by dividing a mass of ten thousand militiamen by ten thousand."

Outcomes of the kind mentioned are the result of ignoring the paramount distinction between member and class and the fact that a class cannot be a member of itself. In all our pursuits, but especially in research, we are constantly faced with the hierarchies of logical levels, so the dangers of level confusions and their puzzling consequences are ubiquitous. The phenomenon of change is no exception; however, it is much more difficult to observe in the behavioral sciences than, for instance, in physics (CHANGE Principles of PROBLEM FORMATION and PROBLEM

RESOLUTION, Watzlawick, Weakland, and Fisch, 1974).

In truth, this is where we are in this puzzling world, where hierarchies in the clergy field should step out of the norm and face the consequences of their mistreatment and disrespect of female clergy, who only want to play their role as God sent and anointed spreaders of the Gospel of Christ. The apostle Paul says it best, in Romans 10:15, "And how shall they preach, except they be sent? As it is written, How beautiful are the feet of them that preach the gospel of peace, and bring glad tidings of good things!"

Let's face it, it has come to the point where women clergy are pointing out the disrespect and division by male clergy. In scripture, God said, "And it shall come to pass afterward, that God will pour out God's Spirit on all flesh; your sons and daughters shall prophesy, your old men shall dream dreams, and your young men shall see visions. Even on the male and female servants in those days, I, God, will pour out my Spirit (Joel 2:28 ESV). "For God shows no partiality." (Romans 2:11 ESV). "But when the Holy Spirit comes, whom I, Christ, will send to you from My Father, the Spirit of Truth, who proceeds from My Father, the Holy Spirit will bear witness about Me. And you will bear witness, because you have been with Me from the beginning" (John 15:26-27 ESV).

To summarize what has been said so far: Group Theory gives us a framework for thinking about the kind of change that can occur within a system that itself stays invariant; the Theory of Logical Types is not concerned with what goes on inside a class, i.e., between its members, but gives us a frame for considering the relationship between member and class and the peculiar metamorphosis which is in the nature of shifts from one logical level to the next higher. If we accept this basic distinction between the two theories, it follows that there are two different types of change. There is one that occurs within a given system, which itself remains unchanged, and one whose occurrence changes the system itself. To exemplify this distinction in more behavioral terms: a person having a nightmare can do many things in his dream–run, hide, fight, scream, jump off a cliff, etc. – but no change from any one of these behaviors to another would ever terminate the nightmare. *We shall henceforth refer to this kind of change as first-order change.* The one way out of a dream involves a change from dreaming to waking. Waking, obviously, is no longer a part of the dream, but a change to an altogether different state. *This type of change will be referred to as second-order change from now on.* Second-order change is thus *change of change*–the very phenomenon whose existence Aristotle denied so categorically.

The Practice of Change/The Problem

Approaching a problem with the aforementioned principles in mind leads to formulating and applying a four-step procedure. The steps are:

1. A clear definition of the problem in concrete terms
2. An investigation of the solutions attempted so far
3. A clear definition of the concrete change to be achieved
4. The formulation and implementation of a plan to produce this change

A Clear Definition of the Problem in Concrete Terms:

There is a very high division or exclusion by male clergy in leadership, who are refusing to ordain anointed women clergy into the pastoral field, to help in spreading the Gospel of Jesus Christ. They refuse to accept God's promise that "all" have been commissioned to prophesy. See Joel 2:28-32, Old Testament, Matthew 28:18-20, and Acts 2:17-21, New Testament.

Who is Affected by this Problem?

Female clergy who had been predestined and anointed by God to come forth and serve by practicing are affected. Romans 10:15, "How beautiful are the feet of those who preach the good news!" It means that the act of spreading good news, or the gospel, is so vital that even the simple act of walking to deliver that message is considered beautiful. Also affected by this problem are congregations and non-believers who want to hear and be saved through these anointed women of God. "And how can he or she hear without a preacher?" Romans 10:14 emphasizes that people cannot learn about God or Jesus unless someone actively preaches the message to them. Essentially, it highlights the importance of sharing the gospel through preaching to reach others with the Christian faith and to mature in it.

What's the Specific Problem?

The problem is male clergy who dishonor God's promised Word by "fighting or kicking against the pricks," which is an idiom that means to fight against something in vain and hurt oneself in the process (Acts 9:5). It can also refer to arguing with people in authority. God has given His women authority to "Go therefore and make disciples of all the nations, baptizing them in the name of the Father and of the Son and of the Holy Spirit, "teaching them to observe all things that I have commanded you; and lo, I am with you always, even to the end of the age." Matthew 28:19-20. So, this problem, gender prejudice, ignoring God's promises, serious clergy role division, embarrassment, isolation, and bullying, deals with principalities in high places. "For we do not wrestle against flesh and blood, but against principalities, against powers, against the rulers of the darkness of this age, against spiritual *hosts* of wickedness in the heavenly *places*." Ephesians 6:12.

As previously outlined earlier the female clergy have gotten ill behind this type of bullying and neglectful treatment. Women preachers, we have never been treated so badly inside the church. All of this treatment breaks one's heart and even messes with the nervous system to behold such actions.

Where and when does this problem occur?

This problem occurs both inside God's place of worship and outside, when visiting other churches, and anytime we gather in Jesus' worship service.

Why is it a significant issue?

It's an issue because of the need for many foot soldiers on the ground for Christ; there is more kingdom building to be done. The kingdom was near in His first advent, but it was rejected by the high Jewish leaders of that time. Christ tore down walls of gender prejudice throughout the New Testament, and He weeps now that men have decided, on their own, to continue their charade.

An Investigation of the Solutions Attempted So Far
(Research the Gap or Need.)

Now that we have identified the problem, we will focus on the next step, which is to research to gain a deeper understanding of the issue. We can talk to people we know who are or could be impacted by this problem. While researching, take notes on aspects of the problem (a particular part or feature) that are within our ability to influence. For example, the financial aspect can be overstressed. There have been many solutions that have been attempted to overcome this division/problem. Some attempted solutions were:

- Discussions of female inclusion as ordained pastors at local, district, and annual conferences

- Discussions of ordaining female priests, bishops, archbishops, and a pope, on a national level
- Panel discussions
- Covert discussions of being more overt
- Leveling the clergy field
- Stop using the word "distraction" when working with your female clergy; there should be no distraction
- Before and during worship service, focus solely on saving souls before the second coming of Christ. We cannot ignore what has become history, because "Those who ignore history, warned Santayana, are doomed to repeat it."

Some General Research Gaps

- Women make up about 12.9% of senior pastor positions in Protestant churches.
- Church size – Churches led by women tend to be small and economically depressed.

- Denominations – Many major denominations, including the Roman Catholic, Southern Baptist, Mormon, and Orthodox churches in America, do not allow women to lead congregations
- History – The United Church of Christ and the Universalists began ordaining women in the 19th century

  NOTE: "Women arguing a point in clergy change." They are attempting to construct a different style of ministry, arguing that women will only truly experience inclusion when <u>change</u> comes in how the Christian faith is organized and symbolized. Some of this transformation is spontaneous and unconscious, some is carefully planned and executed.
- The Seventh-day Adventist church has allowed women to serve in pastoral roles, but the church has been divided on whether to ordain women as pastors.

- In 1990, the Seventh-day Adventist church permitted women to be "commissioned in pastoral ministry."
- In 2015, the Seventh-day Adventist church voted against ordaining women as pastors.
- The church has a history of women serving as Bible instructors and elders in local churches. Some say that the Bible does not support ordaining women as pastors.
- Others say that the Bible does not contain a universal rule against women teaching men.
- Some say that ordination is a work of the Spirit and should not be influenced by Roman Catholic practices.
- Currently, the largest church in the entire global Seventh-day Adventist church is led by a female pastor. Additionally, one of the largest conferences in the North American division, in terms of both numbers and tithes, is led by a female pastor (as of 2/2019).

Jehovah's Witnesses on female pastors/leadership: Only males may be appointed as elders and ministerial servants (their term for deacons). Only baptized males are permitted to officiate at weddings, funerals, and baptisms. A female Witness minister may only lead congregational prayer and teaching in unusual circumstances, and must wear a head covering while doing so.

And, although they don't assume a leadership role within the congregation, they have a full share in the public ministry.

My Research Methodology

To investigate the impact of male and female clergy relations on pastoral inclusion following the printed Bible scripture Joel 2:28, Acts 2:16-18, and Matthew 28:18, my study employed a qualitative and quantitative research paper for informative purposes from online specialists in the faith-based field. Open-ended questions were used during conversations with female clergy, ages 42-69. Scholarly books and academic articles were carefully examined as needed resources.

- Online (with caution)
- Interviews (male and female)
- Scholarly books and articles

A Clear Definition of the Concrete Change to be Achieved

A second-change type is needed in a male-female clergy Christian group. The Holy Spirit will be used as the outside change; Utopia. The goal is for male clergy to, SHUV (Hebrew), repent, bring in the Holy Spirit, you once had to confess your change of:

- Gender prejudice
- Ignoring God's promises
- Serious female clergy role division
- Avoidance

- Embarrassment
- Isolation
- Bullying

Desired State: Describe the desired situation
- Male and female clergy should be able to work together on God's plan of salvation. This will bring in more souls for God's Kingdom. *Selah*
- We share a common characteristic: we are members in Christ. One essential rule, "Whatever involves *all* of a collection must not be one of the collections." We, the members and Christian spirituality being the class, will call upon the Holy Spirit of Christ, eminently, to resolve this problem. The class (Christianity Spirituality) has been running without the guidance or help of the Holy Spirit.
- Hierarchies of the clergy field should step out of the norm and face the consequences of their mistreatment and disrespect of female clergy,

who only want to do their commissioned duty, without fear. Psalm 27:1.

NOTE: An outside source, coming inside the fold of members. The Spirit has been poured out; use it! Joel 2:28; Acts 2:16-18.

The Formulation and Implementation of a Plan to Produce This Change

$A+B = B+A$ (Clergymen plus Clergywomen = Clergywomen and Clergymen)

or

$A+B+(C) = C+A+B$ (Divine Spirit + Clergymen + Clergywoman =

Second-Order Change

(Bringing in an outside source to solve our problem.)

Consequently, no one is totally the same as others, and no one is unique in every respect. Michael Welker, in *God the Spirit*, says that the

Spirit of God gives rise to a multi-place force field that is sensitive to differences. In this force field, the enjoyment of creaturely, invigorating differences can be cultivated, while unjust, debilitating differences can be removed through love, mercy, and gentleness.

People have emphasized over and over again that God's Spirit works union, unanimity, and unity among human beings, indeed that the Spirit "holds together" all that is created. Not only has this been emphasized repeatedly, but it has also been emphasized in connection with the broadest possible variety of interests. Less clarity and energy have been devoted to stating that the "unity of the Spirit" not only tolerates differences and differentiation, but also maintains and cultivates differences that do not contradict justice, mercy, and knowledge of God. According to the prophetic promises whose fulfillment is proclaimed on Pentecost, the Spirit gives rise to a unity that speaks to and includes not only people of the most varied languages witness of women is no less important than that of men, that of the young is no less significant than that of the old, that of the socially disadvantaged is no less relevant than that of the privileged. The promised Spirit of God is effective in that differentiated community, which is sensitive to differences, and in which the differences that stand in opposition to justice, mercy, and knowledge of God are being steadily reduced.

To be sure, in baptism human beings are "baptized into one body" through the Spirit. But the text immediately adds with double emphasis that "Jews or Greeks, slaves or free" have been given the one Spirit to drink and that the unity of the body that arises consists in the interplay of a differentiated diversity that cannot be reduced to a simple unity (1 Corinthians 12:13 and 14ff.).

PART 4: BREACH OF UNITY IN CHRIST

Chapter 9

IMPLEMENTATION OF OUR HOLY SPIRIT

Male Clergy – Jew and Gentile

This proposal is a plea to all male clergy, per our *Holy Spirit*. Male clergy who are in denial of God's promises and plan for predestined and anointed women of God as today's pastors and leaders of Jesus' Commission "To Go." Matthew 28:18; Joel 2:28-29.

Therefore, this plea henceforth welcomes you to the realization that God's promises are not about you only. God loves us "all" (empirically valid). Your unbelief in women as spiritual leaders/pastors of Christ, in this clergy field, is obnoxious and selfish. Men of God, you are holding up barriers that Jesus knocked down centuries ago. The walls or division of man and woman were done away with before Christ's death and after His resurrection. Matthew 28:18 points at no gender, creed, or color. Therefore, we must work together as foot soldiers of Christ, loving and respecting one another.

We, clergy women around the world, give God all glory and honor for choosing us. We are God's light shining through His world that has been tainted with Satan's evilness of deception and division. We gladly request the Holy Spirit to intervene and help male clergy worldwide in their acknowledgment to repent of past and present abuse of the inclusivity of their counterpart, women of God in Christ Jesus.

Specifically, you are hindering the call of God's chosen women of Christ. Namely, as before mentioned, such atrocities as gender biases, gender prejudice, ignoring God's promises concerning "all," serious clergy role division, embarrassment, isolation, and bullying. In other words, a display of misogyny.

We request that you demonstrate your repentance through a "level of hierarchical" change in the Catholic Diocese and the Roman Curia, with increased female inclusion through a level of hierarchical change in the Orthodox Jewish system, and the inclusion of God's female clergy. Furthermore, all Protestant pastoral leaders of the Baptist, Methodist, Trinitarian Pentecostal, and Oneness Pentecostal Churches should also show love and inclusion for all women of God as pastors and leaders of Christ.

Wherefore, as a result of your participation in high principalities, Women clergy have been ridiculed, embarrassed, and demanded to stay in their place, wherever that may be (even Jesus was proud that Mary ignored the kitchen duties and sat at His feet). Repent of your mistreatment.

Nevertheless, it has been resolved that God's chosen clergy of females must "go" and continue in the spreading of the WORD of Christ, anticipating His imminent return.

"GO therefore and make disciples of all the nations, baptizing them in the name of the Father

and of the Son and of the Holy Spirit, teaching them to observe all things that I have commanded you; and lo, I am with you always, even to the end of the age."

Powerfully and unapologetically, repent of your misdeeds toward God's anointed women preaching His Word.

In particular, D. Bonhoeffer addresses the lack of unity in his book, *Communion of Saints*. The Spirit gives rise to a unity in which the prophetic witness of women is no less important than that of men, that of the young is no less significant than that of the old, and that of the socially disadvantaged is no less relevant than that of the privileged. The promised Spirit of God is effective in that differentiated community, which is sensitive to difference, and in which the differences that stand in opposition to justice, mercy, and knowledge of God are being steadily reduced.

But the text immediately adds with double emphasis that "Jew or Greek, slaves or free" have been given the one Spirit to drink, and that the unity of the body that arises consists in the interplay of a differentiated diversity that cannot be reduced to a simple unity (1 Corinthians 12:13-14).

Although this differentiated diversity through the Spirit exists about Christ, it is not arranged according to a hierarchical order among the members themselves. Just as for a body, in some situations, the eyes are particularly important, while in some, the hands are, and still in others, the ears or the feet are vital. The unity issue here is a flexible one that permits many hierarchical structures to coexist and alternate with each other. Unity and equality, in the sense of the interplay of all members, are here bound up with poly-individual diversity and abundance. (*God the Spirit,* Welker). So, my male clergy friends, return, repent, and the Holy Spirit will be revealed in its entirety, but not only for male clergy, but for a globalization of female and male clergy.

Spiritual Proposal for Unified Inclusion
(The Goal Is)

- To stop male clergy, from thinking God only wants you men to spread the Gospel of His Son, Jesus Christ (Joel 2:28-29)
- To make you aware of your distaste for female diversity, treading the same path toward Kingdom building (Isaiah 52:7)
- To have hospitality to all of God's anointed clergy (Genesis 18:1-8)

After your repentance, together we will teach spiritual lessons every quarter, and have the ears of those who in today's world, that do not want to hear what thus saith the Lord. 2 Timothy 4:3 says, "For the time will come when people will not put up with sound doctrine, but instead will gather around them a great number of teachers to say what their itching ears want to hear."

Accordingly, in the name of the Holy Spirit, there will be inclusion of God's women globally, and they will not be questioned or succumb to ridicule or contempt. The unity of the Spirit becomes a reality not by imposing an illusory homogeneity, but by cultivating creaturely differences and by removing unrighteous differences. In other words, we, the female clergy of God, have waited for this time. As the patient sufferers like Job, who acknowledged his hardships in his life, we too see a glimmer of hope. He states that, "All the days of my appointed time will I wait, till my change comes."

Change is the inevitable, unavoidable consequence we believe must happen before God's end-time. As Paul's epistles were sent out, send out your repentance letter of apology by mail, e-mail, crow, or dove to Synagogues, Diocese, Denominational Churches, and Non-Denominational Churches.

Signature

'This is a proposal for 'men' to sign apologizing for the mistreatment and disrespect of God's anointed 'women.' From the non-protection of Satan's high principalities, to the covering up of your lies to God's people concerning women, to your resentment of God allowing His women to carry His Word…

***LORD, I REPENT,** and am wholeheartedly sorry for my abuse of women who acknowledge You as Messiah.*

The Public Person of the Spirit

As a spiritual result, the forgiveness of sins enables not only a "new beginning," but the production of new structural patterns of life. Disintegrated persons and communities are stabilized and regrouped. They are given a new capacity to act. Hard-pressed persons and communities with no firm foothold experience the power of preservation. Old forms of power and domination are replaced. John 14:26 says, "But the Helper, the Holy Spirit, whom the Father will send in My name, He will teach you *all things, and bring to your remembrance all things that I said to you*;" bearers of hope appear unexpectedly and unforeseeably on the scene. Evil spirits and lying spirits, mechanisms of disintegration and destruction, factors that unleash distress, and the vicious circles that form such a tenacious part of that distress are prophetically recognized. They are made accessible to public knowledge by the forgiveness of sins.

All these events can be the first indications that the Spirit of the forgiveness of sins is at work. As we have seen, though, they are in themselves unclear and ambiguous. Prophetic knowledge can remain without effect. People may lack the power to escape the demonic mechanisms that have been recognized. The supposed bearers of hope can prove to be people who make the situation worse. The replacement of one system can lead out of the frying pan and into the fire. "Preservation" can degenerate into a diet of "pie in the sky" and into maintenance of the status quo. The "gathering" of a disintegrated society can become the first step in unleashing new demonic powers. Both for individual persons and for whole societies, sin can unquestionably generate the illusion of deliverance and can hide its operation behind that illusion.

The search for clear knowledge of the Spirit's action, constant prayer for this knowledge, and persistent questioning concerning the criteria of the Spirit's action, over and above superficial displays of power, are indispensable to the knowledge of sin in the light of the power that liberates from sin. According to the testimonies of the prophetic texts and promises, the creation of righteousness and peace was the criterion for the action of the Spirit, who delivers from distress, preserves, renews, mediates knowledge, and forgives sins. On the one hand, the Spirit's action brings help to concrete human beings and enlists the services of actual human beings. On the other hand, the Spirit's action is a process that human beings cannot "make happen," cannot manage, cannot bring under their control. It is a process that accrues to them, that comes upon them, and into which they are drawn.

    The people who are a part of the Spirit's action of forgiving sins and who are affected by this action are not only bearers, but also are borne. They are not only mediators, but also receivers. They not only exercise an influence on their surroundings, but also are affected, strengthened, challenged, and changed by the actions and reactions of others. In this experience of being surrounded and born up, the persons who are renewed by the action of the Spirit and are born up by the process are indeed themselves changed. They are part of this process, and they collaborate in it themselves. This experience of being surrounded and borne up, this uncontrollability of the new beginning established by the forgiveness of sins, this resistance to all attempts to assert the power of "making it happen" – this uncontrollability of the concrete process and experience is accurately described by the expression "rebirth." (Welker)

Thus, as a result, after Christ's death and resurrection, "The sad truth is that the church has lied to women about their worth and value in God's eyes. And I don't believe "lied" is too strong a word. Early Church fathers, and today's Church fathers, "you can break with the sins of your past by admitting them. You must repent for gender prejudice. You must take responsibility for the way you have misrepresented God and His Word to women everywhere."

God's Calling You: The Answer, YES, to HIS CALL!

The answer is YES, to His Call! "Go ye therefore, and teach all nations, baptizing them in the name of the Father, and of the Son, and of the Holy Ghost: Teaching them to observe all things whatsoever I have commanded you: and lo, I am with you always, even unto the end of the world. Amen." Matthews 28:19-20

Personal Witnesses of Their Epiphany

"Chosen to Shepherd: Discovering My True Calling"

From the beginning, my life was intertwined with the struggle for justice and faith. Born to civil rights activists, I was cradled in the heart of the AME church, a denomination birthed out of the fight against racism. The echoes of Black history, and eloquent speeches and sermons demanding freedom and righteousness, were always in the background. I grew up knowing that to believe was to fight, and to have faith was to work for the betterment of our people.

From a young age, I was involved in church life. I served in the youth ministry, sang in the choir, ushered, and even took on roles in the finance committee. I eventually found myself directing youth ministry, teaching Church School, working with the missionary society, and even assisting the pastor directly. On the outside, it seemed I was doing everything one could do for the Lord, but deep down, something felt incomplete. There was a lingering sense of unrest, a whisper that what I was doing, though good, was not the fullness of what I was called to.

Then, unexpectedly, my father passed away. It was as if my life paused for a moment, and I was forced to reflect. In the days and months following his death, my mind became a reel of memories – precious moments of growing up in a household driven by both spiritual and social justice. Oh, how these precious memories flooded my weary soul. I still had so much more to ask of him, to learn from him. He spoke out against every injustice towards humanity. My father's voice, once alive and vibrant, seemed to speak to me through those memories, reminding me of the work he did, the love he showed, and the fire he carried for truth and liberation. It was in that season of grief that God began to speak to me louder than ever before. Proverbs 3:5-6 is what God gave me: "Trust in the Lord with all of thine heart, and lean not on your own understanding; In ALL your ways acknowledge HIM; And HE shall direct your paths."

In my career as a manager, I found myself pastoring my staff without even realizing it. They would come to me with their emotional wounds, spiritual questions, and personal struggles, and I became a shepherd to them in ways I hadn't anticipated. Many of them carried the scars of church hurt and had been injured by leaders who had failed them and by communities that had neglected them. I realized that God was using me in ways I hadn't acknowledged before. It was clear that ministry wasn't just confined to the four walls of the church; it was present in boardrooms, breakrooms, and even in everyday conversations of life.

That realization ignited a deeper hunger within me. I began to seek God earnestly for clarity about what was stirring in my heart. Why did it seem that, despite all I was doing for Him, there was more He was calling me to? As I prayed and sought God's face, it became clearer: God had chosen me to be His mouthpiece, not just in the traditional sense of ministry but in the broken places where people were hurting, in the spaces where injustice needed to be addressed, and in the hearts of those searching for healing.

This call did not come with a title or position, but with a mandate to speak truth and love wherever I found myself. It was a call to be present, to listen, to heal, and to advocate, not just in my church but in every aspect of my life. Through my grief, through the reflection on my father's life, and through shepherding others in unexpected places, I finally came to realize that God had been preparing me all along. I had been chosen to be His voice to the hurting, His hands to the broken, and His presence to the lost. And in that, I found my true calling!

Reverend Linda Roberts Jackson, Chaplain Supervisor

Palliative Care, Trauma & Grief Care, Surgical & Neuro ICU

******MY CALLING BY GOD TO DELIVER HIS MESSAGE******

It was on a Sunday, the 4th Sunday in September 1996. The Spirit of praise and worship was high at Pilgrim Emanuel Missionary Baptist Church in Nashville, Tennessee. Our pastor, Reverend Roderick C. Pounds, Sr., preached a sermon entitled: "The Pull of Sunday Morning!" It came from the book of Luke, the physician, chapter 15, verses 11-32, based on one of Jesus' parables in the Bible, known as The Prodigal Son. It strongly suggests how God reveals Himself in every facet of our lives, like the prodigal son, who lost his way but remembered when he came back. He remembered his father's holy teachings, just like Proverbs 22:6 commands: "To train up a child in the way he should go: and when he is old, he will not depart from it." In other words, the Lord wanted me to recognize Him as being in control, and the redeemer of my soul's salvation.

    The pastor gave example after example of people touched by the redeemer, Jesus, and His mighty power to heal, deliver, and set free. I was included. Every witness pulled my heart to hear the voice of God. And, before I knew it, during the invitation to discipleship, I was pulled from my seat. And when the pastor asked me, 'What brought you up?' I opened my mouth and these words came forth: "The Lord has called me to deliver His message of what thus says the Lord," followed by tears streaming from my eyes and loud utterances and shouts of praise!

Later that day, after coming down from a spiritual high, I found myself questioning my calling. However, every doubting feeling was filled by an epiphany through the manifestation of Christ (Matthew 2:1-12). Yes, a real-life experience of His sovereignty. Even in my dreams, I could see myself preaching, and I would wake up drenched in sweat.

Oh, what a mighty God I serve! Hallelujah, and thank You, Jesus!

Reverend and Evangelist JoAnne Harris, Th.B., Associate Minister

Heaven's View Baptist Church

FAITH for LIFE

It was at First Church in Gary, Indiana, that I first met Reverend Elizabeth Burnett. She sat in a chair over in a space beside a table while we lined up to get lunch at a Sunday School Convention, where I attended as a delegate from Wayman Chapel in Kokomo, Indiana. She was looking in my direction, and told me to come to her. I didn't know her, so I thought she might be talking to someone else whom she knew, so I just turned my head and looked forward. She said, "I am talking to you!" So, after I confirmed that she meant me, I went over to see what she wanted.

"God's got something he wants you to do," she said. "I don't know who you are, but the Lord showed you to me and pointed you out to me. He told me to tell you that He has something for you to do. So, what are you doing?" Have you ever had someone ask you a question that you wished they wouldn't ask, because you don't feel like you have the right answer? Well, I finally mustered up the courage to say, "I am teaching Sunday School," to which she replied, "No, that's not it."

Then I said, feebly, "I teach Sunday School." She said, "No, that's not it." Finally, she said, "I don't know what it is, but it may be a ministry like mine is." Rev. Burnett said, "I don't know why I am still here. Over a year ago, I was given up to die, and my family was called in, but for some reason, God spared me. I was ready to go home, but God kept me here, and I have wondered why ever since. Perhaps God has kept me here to share this with you, as you may be the one to take my place at Hills Chapel. I don't know, I just know He showed me that I had to tell you this when I saw you in line today. You stay close to Him, and He will reveal to you what it is."

I walked away thinking, I don't know what to make of this, but it sure is strange that a woman preacher would call me out in an AME Church School convention to give me a message like that. This marked the beginning of a journey that has spanned twenty-eight years, bringing me back to the first church where I was assigned as pastor about four or five years after meeting Rev. Burnett. The year she passed away, I was the person assigned here to take her place. I never told anyone in authority, and I am sure she never told anyone either. It was our secret, and we watched to see how God would work out His will in Hills Chapel, this little Church in Weaver, Indiana, a little Christian named Vivian, and a preacher named Rev. Elizabeth Burnett.

    Initially, I couldn't see how God could use me. After all, there were so many others I could think of who I thought would fit the bill. I didn't even keep up with Rev. Burnett. I saw her that time and went on my way until the next time another preacher called me out, and said basically the same thing that she had said. Within about a year, three preachers had pointed me out and given me the same message. Then God spoke to me. Because you can't go on what someone else says when it comes to your faith walk, you have to have an encounter yourself.

I trusted the Lord Jesus Christ as my personal Savior at the age of 14, according to church records. But when I was a child, I knew there was more to life than just living each day and then finally one day dying to nothingness. I knew very soon that I was not the nicest person you ever wanted to meet. My sins weighed heavily on my mind. I hated the person I sometimes was, and couldn't figure out how to carry out my good intentions. I knew what I deserved when I looked into my heart. It was this discontent that led me to cling to the message that there was hope, for even a sinner like me.

I went to church next door to my home, Guildfield Baptist Church, where I heard it said that "God so loved the world that He gave His only begotten Son, that whosoever believeth on Him should not perish, but have everlasting life." Before I realized my sinful condition, the songs of the church didn't mean that much to me. As a matter of fact, sometimes they annoyed me. That was before the age of accountability. Then, when I began to be bothered by my sins, I was looking for someone or something to help me out of this wretched condition that I found myself in. I needed a Savior and hope. John 5:24 says, "Most assuredly, I say to you he who hears My word and believes in Him who sent Me has everlasting life, and shall not come into judgement, but has passed from death unto life." That's what I wanted, and that's what I needed. I wasn't the smartest person you would ever meet, but I knew I had a sin problem. No one had to hold me over the fire; I just knew.

    I feel that we all know. We know when we aren't what we should be. We know the battle we have with sin. Paul the apostle said, "The thing that I want to do, I don't do, and the thing that I don't want to do, I do. O wretched man that I am, who shall deliver me from this body of death?"

It was not the Holy Spirit that I sought; it wasn't understanding that it was salvation. Some folks want to understand everything before they accept Christ as their personal savior. Let me cue you in on a secret. Even after you are born again, you will not understand everything, and even when you are old and grey, you won't understand everything. There are two things to understand about God: life and Christianity. However, the good news is that understanding is not a requirement for salvation; faith is.

It took faith for me to be saved. It took faith for me to grow in Christ; it took faith for me to believe that I had anything to offer in the Church. It took faith for me to get back up after I made my first mistakes as a Christian, and guess what? It takes faith for me to get back up when I fall now. An eight-ounce glass reminds me of my faith walk. I want to share a little story with you.

One day, Bishop Mayo was sitting in the dining room after dinner with some other ministers. Those that I called the big shots, since the group consisted of the presiding elders and ministers of our largest churches in the district. This incident occurred at one of our annual conferences held at St. John in Indianapolis, Indiana. "I think she can carry this out," said Bishop Mayo. "Reverend," he said, "Would you take this glass and fill it with water?" "Yes, Bishop, I will," I replied. Then he continued, "I want you to just have it filled to about right here, no ice, and just tap water, not ice water, please." "Yes, sir, Bishop," I said, and I went to get it. The kitchen was crowded with people, and I had to ask for a glass of water.

"Excuse me, could I have a glass half full of tap water for the Bishop?" I asked. "Sure," a lady replied and proceeded to get the water. As she walked off, she said, "I will just add a little ice to it." I said, "No! The Bishop said he just wants tap water, no ice, and only half full." "Well, I will give him cold water out of the refrigerator," she said. "No! I said again, "Just tap water." "Well, why does he only want it half full?" she said in an agitated tone. "That doesn't make sense." I don't know what I said, but I knew I had to get it half full of tap water, no ice, and take it to him. She was fully irritated with the request by now, but she grudgingly gave me the glass half full of tap water to take back, and of course, not without expressing her feelings.

When I took the water back, the bishop said, "Thank you, I finally got what I asked for." To the other ministers, he said, "You all don't know how many times I have asked for this and gotten a glass full, or ice water, and even sometimes Kool-Aid, anything but what I asked for." Then he reached into his briefcase and brought out an Alka-Seltzer, dropping it in. "Thanks," he said. "You have been a big help."

Faith is like that. Hebrews states in Chapter 11:1, "Now faith is the substance of things hoped for, the evidence of things not seen." I didn't see why he wanted half a glass of water. We can't see what God has in mind for us before we are saved. We can't see what Heaven looks like, nor can we see what lies ahead for us in this life. It means that we must step out on faith, to see beyond our present state and to trust God. I trusted Him, by faith I saw my sins on the cross, by faith I submitted myself to the body of believers to grow up, and by faith I surrendered my life to him in service. It's a good journey, and He's the sweetest friend I know!

Take my life and let it be, consecrated Lord to Thee.

Take my hands and let them move
At the impulse of Thy love, At the impulse of Thy love.

Pastor Vivian Snardon, Retired
Pastored Seven AME Churches

Chosen by GOD

I believe it was back in 1986. I acknowledged that God found me. What do I mean? God opened my spiritual eyes so that I could see His Son as my Lord and Savior. I knew God the Father, but I had not accepted Jesus Christ into my heart. When I had my first miscarriage, I did not question God as to what happened or what went wrong. I knew it had to happen for a reason, but I didn't know what that reason was at the time. I begin to draw closer to God. I started reading more of the Word, and in doing so, I had more questions. I had church friends whom I could ask questions to, since they were more spiritually mature than I was. As I read and received answers to my questions, my heart began to open to Jesus entering.

I was brought up in the church; however, I did not know Christ as my Lord and Savior until I was about 25 or 26 years old. When Christ came into my heart, I realized I had to forgive some people as well as ask for forgiveness. I started my journey by going to one person whom I knew I did not like, and she did not like me. However, because I was so excited to have Christ in my life, I didn't have a problem with asking for forgiveness. I shared my experience with the Lord and the person and apologized for any wrongdoing. It felt so good to be obedient to God. This is the moment when I preach, share, or proclaim the word of God.

Evangelist Terrie L. Nelson
Cathedral of Praise Church of God In Christ

In conclusion, let us agree with the Gamaliel approach, as outlined in Acts 5:34-39, as Schenck (*a male witness*) points out in his book, *A Biblical Argument for Women in Ministry and Leadership.* If women in ministry are not of God, it will go nowhere. But if it is of God, you will find yourself fighting God.

When a woman believes that God is calling her to ministry, don't stand in her way. Open up doors for her and see what the Lord wants to do. When the Holy Spirit lights a fire, don't try to put it out!

Whatever you do, don't harden your heart. It is human nature to double down. We sometimes know deep down that we are wrong, but we don't even let our conscious minds consider it. We double down and harden our hearts without reflecting on whether we are actually doing the right thing. We stubbornly dig a deeper and deeper hole for ourselves, often with the most ingenious and brilliant-sounding intellectual arguments. We are wearing no clothes, but we come up with the most incredible arguments to prove that we are.

"Today, if you hear his voice, don't harden your hearts" (Hebrews 3:7). When God raises a Deborah, fight with her. When God raises a Huldah, seek out her discernment. When God raises a Priscilla, let her disciple you. When God raises a Phoebe, let her minister to you. And whatever you do, in word or deed, do it all in the name of the Lord Jesus.

A SENSE OF BEING

LORD, thank You for my spirituality; my experience of developing a sense of meaning, purpose, and morality. I looked for you and I found you, hallelujah! LORD, you have given me a sense of identity, a sense of belonging, a sense of holiness. My sisters and brothers need Your holy touch, your Spirit of doveness, to rest upon them, that their eyes may be opened to what your Spirit can provide. With open eyes, they can see the purpose in life, that You, Oh LORD, have for them, hallelujah. The purpose to crawl out of the barrel and pull another brother or sister up with them; go back down in the barrel and pull another sister or brother up. Let our spirituality move someone toward the kingdom of heaven, where Your glory lies.

My thankful revelation of Christ, His Father, and the Holy Spirit, Hallelujah!
Reverend Janet L. Seay, 9/15/2009.

MY PRAYER OF CHANGE

LORD help me to surrender in that split-second moment when I'm presented with a choice. Fill me with Your power to resist, steady my feet to stand firm, and accept Your power to activate change. In Jesus' name I pray. Amen.

BIBLIOGRAPHY

10 Lies the Church Tells Women
    J. Lee Grady, Charisma House Book Group. Lake Mary, Florida, 2006

A Biblical Argument for Women in Ministry and Leadership
    Ken Schenck, Lulu.com. Coppell, Texas. 2024

Christ-Centered Exposition
    Tony Merida, B&H Publishing Group. Brentwood, Tennessee. 2021
    "Doriani." p. 164

Taking Heaven by Storm
    John H. Wigger. NY: Oxford University Press, Inc. 1998

"Anointed Women and Their Role in Ministry"
    Cindy Sears (article). October 18, 2015.

"Women, Gentiles, and the Messianic Mission in Matthew's Genealogy"
    John C. Hutchison, Article. Biblio. Theca Sacra: Vol. BSAC 158:630. April 2001

"The Five Women in Matthew's Genealogy"
    J. C. Weren. Journal: Catholic Biblical Quarterly 59 (April 1997): p. 288

"The Four (Five) Women and Other Annotations in Matthew's Genealogy"
    New Testament Studies 43 (1997): 527

Genealogies of Jesus Christ and the Gospel, ed.

James Hastings (New York: Scribner's Sons, 1907), p. 638.

"The Women in Matthew's Genealogy"
Edwin D. Freed. Journal for the Study of the New Testament 29 (1987): pgs. 3-19

"The Scriptures of the Prologue to St. Matthew's Gospel"
Helen Milton, Journal of Biblical Literature 81 (1962): p. 176

The Birth of the Messiah
(Garden City, NY: Doubleday, 1997), 64-74 and Freed, and *The Women in Matthew's Genealogy,*" p. 4

"The Women in Jesus's Family Tree"
Theology 97 (1994): p. 418

The Purpose of the Biblical Genalogies
2d ed. (Cambridge: Cambridge University Press, 1988), pgs. 176-79

A Critical and Exegetical Commentary on the Gospel According to Saint Matthew
W. D. Davies and Dale C. Allison. International Critical Commentary (Edinburgh: Clark,
1988), 1:170

Tamar's Ancestry and Rahab's Marriage: Two Problems in the Matthean Genealogy
Novum Testamentum 37 (1995): 314-320.

The Shepherd's Notes, Romans
Dana Gould. B&H Publishing; Nashville, Tennessee 1998

Her Story: Women in Christian Tradition (2nd Edition)
    Barbara J. MacHaffie. Minneapolis, MN: Augsburg Fortress Publishers, 2006

Not Without a Struggle
    Bishop Vashti Murphy McKenzie. The Pilgrim Press, Cleveland, Ohio. 1996

Jesus and Woman: An Exciting Discovery of What He Offered Her
    Lisa Sergio. EPM Publications, Inc., McLean, Virginia, 1975

Journey to the Well
    Bishop Vashti Murphy McKenzie. Penguin Compass. New York, New York. 2003.
    Bid, Sergio. 104-05. "Scavius"
    Saint Hildegard of Bingen, 1098-1179. Paulist Press, Mahwah, New Jersey. 1990

"JESUS and WOMAN: WHAT DID JESUS DO?
    Joe E. Trull. Journal: Priscilla Papers. Vol: pp 14:2 (Spring 2000)

The Invisible War
    Chip Ingram. Baker Publishing Group. Grand Rapids, Michigan. 2015

A Woman's Place
    Katelyn Beaty. Howard Books. NY, NY. 2016

Change – Principles of Problem Formation and Problem Resolution
    Paul Watzlawick, John Weakland, and Richard Fisch. W. W. Norton and Company.
    NY, NY. 1974.

God the Spirit
    Michael Welker. Fortress Press. Minneapolis, MN. 1994.

www.ingramcontent.com/pod-product-compliance
Lightning Source LLC
Chambersburg PA
CBHW050148170426
43197CB00011B/2013